ECTON NOT UNMINDFUL

The men of a Northamptonshire Village
1914-1918

Angela Crabtree

2013

RWMRG PUBLICATIONS

RWMRG Publications
www.raundswarmemorials.org

ISBN: 978-0-9556541-4-5

Grafton (Northampton) Limited
Printers and Designers
Northampton NN1 2PT

Front Cover: Ecton Shrine
Inside Front: Architect's sketch of Ecton Shrine
Back Cover: Roll of Honour of Ecton Men who served their
Country in the Great War.

CONTENTS

ACKNOWLEDGEMENTS

For all matters military I am indebted to both **Chris Holland** and **Roger Storey.** Chris for his unfailing patience and unstinting efforts to answer questions and queries no matter how slight. Also for researching facts around the deaths of some of the men and allowing me to include these accounts in the book. Roger for helping with all aspects of the Northamptonshire Regiment and his cheerfulness whilst doing so. (This was most apparent on days the Northampton Saints Rugby Team won a match). Also I have to thank **Chris Baker** and **Paul Webster**, both members of the Heart of England branch of the Western Front Association, with their help in coming to the rescue with answers that eluded both Chris and myself.

For sharing their memories of the village and the men who returned after the war I am grateful to **Suie Rands, Betty Cunningham, Vera Middleton** and **Geoff Harlott,** all sadly deceased since I began research into the lives of the men. My thanks also go to **David Dicks, Rodney Ingram, Jean Haycox, Sylvia and Brian Saunders, Jean Leigh, Marion Gleave** and **Kath Busby**, for their enthusiasm for the project, their family memories and permission to use diaries and photographs. The book would not have started without the **U3A WW1 Group** and the help of **Shena** and **David Humphries** who were instrumental in urging me to follow the history of the men on the Ecton Shrine/War Memorial.

My task was made easier by the assistance of the staff of the **Northampton Record Office** and **Jon-Paul Carr** and **the staff of the Northampton Central Library**. Also the hard work put in by **Chris Hewitt** who due to her experience in local newspaper offices, enabled her to spot many things which had slipped through the 'net' whilst proof-reading the script. Also to **Steve** and **Maggie Bence** (RWMRG Publications) who agreed to publish the book and gave a great deal of help and advice during the process.

Nothing would have progressed beyond research into the men who died without the unstinting help and support of my husband, **Jim Crabtree**, who magically changed very poor photographs into clear images and sorted out the computer 'glitches' which seemed to occur with horrible frequency. He also spent hours with me in graveyards in Belgium, France and England and in record offices and libraries where once again his skill with the camera saved many hours of hand-copying documents.

Angela Crabtree 2013.

THE VILLAGE

Ecton is a small village in Northamptonshire, situated halfway between Northampton and Wellingborough, with currently around four hundred inhabitants. At the time the First World War started there were around five hundred people living and working there. The Ecton Estate, which had provided generations of Ecton villagers with employment, passed by marriage, in 1881 from the Isted family to the Sotheby family who continued to live there until 1954.

I hope to give a glimpse into the lives of the men of Ecton, who, taking up arms, were in many cases leaving their homes for the first time. Many had been under the patronage of the Ecton Estate; farm workers, and servants from Ecton Hall together with the village tradesmen, wheelwrights, blacksmiths and bakers, all united in their efforts to save a way of life they knew from being overrun by an enemy force. Little did they realise when they left to fight that they were leaving behind a pattern of life which, after the war, would be a changing one. Although many of them would return to their farms and fields, very slowly the life they had known would be eroded away. Twenty years after they had gone forth to fight in "the war to end all wars" their sons would be picking up weapons and following in their footsteps to fight the same enemy.

In the First World War eighty-four men from the village joined the armed forces and their names are recorded on an illuminated Roll of Honour in the Church of St. Mary Magdalene. The Church is situated in Church Way, opposite the Georgian Rectory and just outside the gates of Ecton Hall. There is a Shrine/War Memorial in the village to the men who died whilst on Active Service and a book compiled by Reverend Canon Jephson which was kept in the church. (Referred to in the text as The Ecton War Book).

THE SHRINE/WAR MEMORIAL

Situated at the fork of the Northampton and Wellingborough Roads, in a suitably prominent place, is a covered continental style shrine, 12 feet high and constructed of Duston stone and oak grown on the Ecton estates. It is roofed in oak and covered with hand-made Brosley tiles. The original architect Mr. Gerald Horsley died before the work was completed and it was taken over by Mr. Arthur Keen F.R.I.B.A., the builder was Mr.J.Higgs of Northampton.

The inscription carved on the beam across the front of the shrine under the cross provided the title for this book. It reads:

"Ecton Not Unmindful, 1917"

The Northampton Independent carried a report on October 20th 1917 covering the dedication of the shrine by the Bishop of Peterborough. Commemorating: **Lionel Frederick Southwell Sotheby (Black Watch), Geoffrey Stopford-Sackville (Royal Navy), Edgar Hensman, Horace Hensman, Harry E. Tipler, Samuel Dexter, Ralph E. Elson, Sidney G.A.Brown** and **Andrew Wood**. On a parallel Roll of Honour was inscribed **Edgar Robert Mobbs**, *"Farewell to you brave and gallant gentleman"* (from Lord Spencer's speech at Northampton August 4 1917). The inclusion of Edgar R. Mobbs, D.S.O, though not an Ecton man was at the special request of Mrs. Sotheby.

The interior inscription on the Shrine is *"Of your Charity pray for the souls of those who gave their lives for you"*. On the wall at the back of the crucifix *"Rest eternal grant them O Lord and let light perpetual shine upon them"*.

The Shrine was erected in 1917, paid for by Mrs. Sotheby and given to the village as a gift. This information was given in the Northampton Independent newspaper report of the dedication. It was not recorded in the Parish Council records and when the Shrine was refurbished in 1977/8 there was a doubt as to who was responsible for its upkeep.

In 1948 the Parish Council was advised of an amendment of the law relating to War Memorials contained in the Local Government Act. The question of looking after the garden around the Memorial was discussed in 1952 and left unanswered at that time. In 1973 members of the Youth Club were asked if they would agree to clean the spaces in front of the Memorial which had become overgrown with weeds. In July 1975 the Parish Council at that time were unsure who was responsible for the upkeep of the memorial and had applied to Messrs. Fisher & Co., the Agents for the Ecton Estates, whether or not it was their responsibility. Having not had a response the September Parish Council meeting of the same year asked the Clerk to confirm with the Agents that they would have no objection if the Parish Council assumed responsibility for the upkeep and maintenance of the Memorial as they were greatly concerned about the state it had fallen into. They also decided to hold a Parish Meeting on 20th October 1975 at 7.30pm in order the public could decide on what action should be taken with regard to its repair and maintenance.

In October 1975 Messrs. Fisher & Co. stated they were not prepared to undertake any work on the Memorial and had no objections to the structure being taken over by the Parish Council if it was the will of the Parish. At the public meeting it was resolved that the Parish Council be asked to accept full responsibility for any repair and maintenance.

The Chairman reminded the meeting that a certain amount of vandalism had taken place over the years and it was now the responsibility of the Parish to decide what action should be taken and consideration should be given as to whether it should be demolished, or moved to a better site less likely prone to vandalism or that the Memorial should be repaired and maintained on its proper site.

It was resolved that the Parish Council be asked to obtain expert advice on the possibility of the structure being so altered so as not to afford shelter to the youth of the village. The Meeting appealed to the youths present for their help in ensuring that the Memorial is properly cared for and to influence the younger generation by their own actions.

24th November 1975 Mr.D.Cox, Architect, was welcomed to the Parish Council meeting. Mr. Cox had offered to examine the possibility of amending the existing structure of the Shrine with a view to discouraging the present misuse and vandalism. It appeared that the main attraction in its present form is the shelter it affords when it rains, and if this was removed and sufficient of the roof retained to form a canopy protection to the cross and to the role of honour, it would no doubt go some way to lessening the appeal of the building as a meeting place during inclement weather. Mr. Cox pointed out that he had incorporated the existing gable in a new position a feature he considered should be retained together with the general outline of the building. He pointed out in his view that the existing structure was of such regular symmetrical shape that it was a pity anything at all needed to be done to it but he understood the concern of the Parish Council and prepared his sketch with this in mind. After some discussion it was agreed that Mr. Cox should endeavour to incorporate a slight modification to the retaining walls at the side of the steps and also to obtain an estimate of the cost of the work for the consideration of the Parish Council.

On the 29th March 1976, Mr. Cox attended again and he advised that he had looked again at the various alternatives for altering the Memorial and each time he came back to a version of the original structure. He felt that to reduce the profile in anyway which changed the general existing shape, would be entirely wrong. Or it should be kept at least as the sketch produced at the last meeting. All other attempts to redesign it would be quite radical and in consequence expensive. Even if this course was adopted, the effect would not in his view justify the expense. He apologised for being negative but considered the scheme originally prepared the only reasonable solution, subject to minor amendments. Other than to retain the existing building and repair, Mr. Cox estimated that the cost of the scheme would be in the region of £600-£750.

A suggestion was made to retain the existing structure and to provide a pair of ornamental wrought-iron gates at the entrance to the roofed section. Mr. Cox thought this to be an idea worth investigating.

The Clerk was asked to obtain a quotation from Mr. Brown of Brown and Moule, Mears Ashby for the supply and fixing of a pair or ornamental wrought-iron gates.

On the 17th September 1976 Fisher & Co. wrote to the Parish Council to confirm that they had some of the same sort of tile in store, which they would be pleased to supply free of charge to the Parish Council, so that the roof of the Memorial could be repaired. The Clerk is to advise the Agents as soon as the Parish Council is in in a position to start the work and to thank Fisher & Co. for their kind offer.

The following year the Clerk referred to a grant of £250 which had been included in the Borough Council's capital programme for 1977/78 towards the cost of refurbishing and he also submitted drawings of various types of ornamental gates which would be made by Brown & Moule, The Forge, Bakehouse Lane, Mears Ashby. It was agreed that Brown & Moule be asked to supply and fix a pair of ornamental gates based on the design referred to in their catalogue as No.1560 and to allow for an opening of only 6 inches from the top of the gates to the underside of the roof of the Memorial. It was hoped that the gates would be completed by the end of July 1977.

At the Parish Council meeting November 1977 George Rands, Chairman, reported that the wrought-iron gates had been installed at the War Memorial, the roof repaired and the two small gardens had been planted with flowers. The work on the roof was carried out by the Chairman in conjunction with Mr. Latham who also planted the flowers. The two small beds were cleared and cultivated under arrangements made by the Vice-Chairman. The meeting expressed their thanks for the actions taken. The Chairman also reported that the Rector had offered to have the Crucifix taken down, cleaned and treated and this was accepted. It was resolved to obtain a quotation for the provision of a new Roll of Honour on wood with gold leaf lettering.

In January 1978 Mr.D.M.Kightley of 53, Park Road, Wellingborough, was asked to arrange for the Rolls of Honour to be prepared, using the existing oak panels and for the names of the fallen to be reproduced in gold leaf as they appeared on the originals. In March the Clerk submitted the new Rolls of Honour prepared by Mr. Kightley, including the names of the eighteen persons who had fallen in the 1914-18 Great War. (Mr. Kightley mis-read the initials of Sidney Brown and he is on the Shrine as S.O.A.Brown and should have been S.G.A.Brown). Interestingly the Shrine must have undergone a renovation and possibly a re-dedication prior to 1977 as nine more names of village men were recorded since the original dedication and Edgar Mobbs was removed. No record has been found of when the change was made. The 1977 refurbishment replaced what the Parish Council saw at the time on the Rolls of Honour.

The rolls were to be re-fixed within the Shrine along with the Crucifix, which had been cleaned up by the Rector and kept in his garage for safe-keeping. A missing inscription was also to be replaced. David Dicks remembers walking through the village with George Rands, carrying the crucifix and the other pieces and taking them from George's workshop, where they had been repaired and putting them back on the Shrine. The metal gates and the window bars are still in situ today.

By April 1978, the re-dedication of the Shrine/War Memorial had been discussed with the Rector Canon H.F.Cyprian Thorpe and it was decided that arrangements be made for this to be held on 23rd July 1978 at 10.30am. A Sub-committee consisting of George Rands (Chairman of Parish Council), Mr.Dicks and Mrs. Johnson, was formed to carry out all the arrangements. Mr.E.S. Needham offered to notify the local press of the arrangements so that publicity could be given in the week prior to the 23rd July. The Chairman and Mr. Dicks were authorised to arrange for the provision of some form of protection for the Memorial roof. At the following meeting of the Council the Chairman reported on the action taken by the sub-committee in connection with the Service of Re-dedication of the Memorial to be conducted by the Rector, Canon Thorpe, The Worshipful, the Mayor of the Borough of Wellingborough, (Councillor Mrs.P.Ritchie) and members of the County Branch and Local Branches of the Royal British Legion had also agreed to attend.

Mrs.I.L.Palmer of 25, Eden Close, Northampton had written to enquire if the name of her father, the late Thomas Frank Barrick, an Ecton resident who fought in WW1 could be added to the Roll of Honour. She was informed that the roll only relates to the men from the village who gave their lives whilst on Active Service.

On 28th July a letter was received from the Mayor of the Borough of Wellingborough, thanking the Parish Council for inviting her to such a pleasant ceremony on Sunday morning the 23rd July. Shortly afterwards the Police were informed that the locks to the ornamental gates had been smashed. The Council arranged for replacements. On Remembrance Sunday 12th November 1978 a service was held at the Shrine and a poppy wreath was supplied by the Borough Council.

The Shrine/War Memorial underwent a second refurbishment in 1999 when David Dicks was Chairman of the Parish Council and the work was carried out by Mr. A.D.Stone.

A short and moving service is held around the Shrine at 11am every Remembrance Sunday and attended by almost all the village. Before the two minute silence is held, the Chairman of the Parish Council solemnly reads the names of the eighteen men who died.

Permission to quote from the article given in the Northampton Independent Newspaper was given by David Summers of the Northampton Newspapers Group.

12

THE TWO PLAQUES ON THE SHRINE

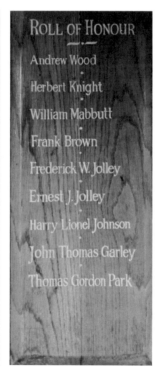

ROLL OF HONOUR

Lionel Frederick-Southwell Sotheby

Geoffrey W. Stopford-Sackville

Edgar H. Hensman

Horace A. Hensman

Harry E. Tipler

Samuel Dexter

Bertie Timms

Ralph E. Elson

Sydney O. A. Brown

ROLL OF HONOUR

Andrew Wood

Herbert Knight

William Mabbutt

Frank Brown

Frederick W. Jolley

Ernest J. Jolley

Harry Lionel Johnson

John Thomas Garley

Thomas Gordon Park

THE ECTON WAR BOOK

A book of photographs, compiled by Canon Arthur William Jephson, Rector (1908-1935) was placed by him in the church. He started the book in 1914 when the first men from the village enlisted. It contains photographs of most of the men with details of their regiments, their involvement with the church and comments on the death or discharge of many of them. Of the 18 men who were killed 15 appear in this book.

Of the three men who were not in the book, two were Ecton men who had moved away from the village before they enlisted and the third a man from Kettering who was step-brother to a village man. Although mainly detailing the village inhabitants the book also records friends and relations of the Sotheby family and Canon Jephson. In 1919 the completed book was sent away to be bound before being placed in the church. The original has now been donated, for safekeeping, to the Northamptonshire County Record Office with a copy being kept in the church in Ecton for visitors to look at. (In the following text Canon Jephson's book will be referred to as the Ecton War Book.)

It is much easier to trace the history of the men who died during the war due to the availability of the Commonwealth War Graves records, but sadly not as easy to follow the lives of the men who returned. Consequently some personal histories are very short but that does not diminish the contribution they made both in their service to their Country and to village life.

PART 1

THE MEN WHO DIDN'T RETURN

The Eighteen Men Remembered on the Shrine

"ECTON NOT UNMINDFUL"

BROWN, Francis W.	Northamptonshire Regiment
BROWN, Sydney G. A.	Northamptonshire Regiment
DEXTER, Samuel	Northampton Regiment
ELSON, Ralph E.	Essex Regiment
GARLEY, John T.	Royal Engineers
HENSMAN, Edgar H.	Middlesex Regiment
HENSMAN, Horace A.	Bedfordshire Regiment
JOHNSON, Harry L.	Canadian Infantry
JOLLEY, Ernest J.	Bedfordshire Regiment
JOLLEY, Frederick W.	London Regiment
KNIGHT, Herbert	Royal Fusiliers
MABBUTT, William	Leicester Regiment
PARK, Thomas G.	Royal Naval Volunteer Reserve
SOTHEBY, Lionel F. S.	Argyll & Sutherland Highlanders
STOPFORD-SACKVILLE, Geoffrey W.	Royal Navy
TIMMS, Bertie	Middlesex Regiment
TIPLER, Harry Edward	Royal Engineers
WOOD, Andrew	Royal West Surrey Regiment

FRANCIS WILLIAM BROWN (1896-1917)

Francis, known as Frank, was one of the bell ringers, who enlisted during the war. His name is on a plaque hanging in the Belfry, referred to in the local paper as "The Patriotic Bell Ringers".

Frank enlisted in the recruitment office in Northampton in October 1914. He was five feet four and a half inches tall and his apparent age was given as nineteen years and seven months. His physical development was poor, however he was considered fit for the Territorial Force and went into the 4th Battalion Northamptonshire Regiment (Private 205).

On 27th April 1915 he was transferred to the 54th East Anglian Divisional Cyclist Company (Private 18065). The Division sailed on the 30th July 1915 from Devonport on H.M.Troopship *Royal George* and was transhipped to the H.M.Troopship *Osmanieh* landing at Lemnos on 15th August, finally disembarking at Suvla Bay on 16th to form part of the Gallipoli campaign. On the 10th February 1916 Frank received eight days Field Punishment No.2 for being seen drunk in town at 9.20pm. On 21st June 1916 he embarked on H.M.Troopship *Egra* as part of a draft to the 13th Divisional Cyclist Company who sailed to Basrah. (Basra, Iraq).

Frank died of smallpox in December 1917. According to his service records, a wire was received by the War Record Office in London on 12th December, stating he had died, another wire was sent back to Basrah asking them to confirm that the report of death definitely referred to Francis William Brown, 13th Divisional Cyclist Company late (Private 205) Northampton Regiment. Also a telegraph was received from John Brown, his father, to the War Records Office asking for further news as he had received a telegraph saying Frank was ill with smallpox. He was informed that Frank had died, and on 28th June 1918 the family received Frank's identity disc and silver watch (of Turkish workmanship). At the time of Frank's death John and Ada Brown were living at North Lodge, Ecton. On the 1st May 1919 John Brown signed a declaration for the army records, that he, his wife, sons Alfred Reginald Brown, Arthur Leonard Brown and daughters, Nora Annie Brown and Florence Irene Brown were all living at North Lodge, Ecton, and were Francis' nearest relations. This form was witnessed by Canon Arthur W. Jephson, Ecton Rectory, upon receipt of which the War Office sent a scroll and bronze plaque to the family. This was issued to families of the war dead. (See Service Medal Appendix). Frank is buried in Baghdad (North Gate) War Cemetery. The cemetery was begun in April 1917 and has been enlarged since the end of the First World War. There are 4,160 casualties commemorated in the cemetery, together with 2,729 unidentified burials.

The Northampton Independent newspaper reported:
Cyclist Francis William Brown, of the 13th Division Cyclist Corps, eldest son of Mr. and Mrs. John Brown of North Lodge, Ecton and fiancé of Miss Willis of Moulton, is reported to have died of smallpox in Mesopotamia on the 10th December 1917, having been in the East for over two years. It also reported that originally he had joined the Northampton Territorials in September 1914 and served with them in the Dardanelles. Prior to his joining up he had been working with Messrs. Wright Brothers of The Mounts, Northampton. The report concluded with the information that another of his brothers, Reginald, was serving in France.

SIDNEY GEORGE ALBERT BROWN (1896-1915)

Photograph courtesy of Northamptonshire Newspapers

In 1901 Sidney was living in Ecton with his Grandparents, William and Sarah Fennell. His widowed mother had remarried in 1899, and was living in Kettering with her second husband Stephen Wood. She had just given birth to Mary Alice the first of Sidney's four half-sisters; he also had an elder brother Charles and a younger sister Ethel Frances. Stephen Wood also had children, including Andrew who is remembered on the Ecton Shrine, and who was the 'Unknown' who started my investigation.

Sidney enlisted in the 2nd Battalion, Northamptonshire Regiment, (Private 14271), at Kettering on 31st August 1914. Although part of his service record still exists, it is mainly illegible. Sufficient survives however for the comment: Missing on 9th May 1915, next of kin informed on 10th June 1915 and then more than a year later, on the 9th October 1916, his Mother was finally notified of his death.

Sidney rose from Private to Lance Corporal but was reduced back to Private on 16th April 1915 for misconduct. On the service record it states that his brother, Charles Brown age 21, is a Sergeant but due to damage to the record it is impossible to see which Regiment he was serving in.

The 2nd Battalion of the Regiment was a regular army battalion that had been serving in Alexandria. When war was declared the Battalion sailed back to England arriving in October 1914 and went on to Winchester where it joined the 24th Brigade, 8th Division. (The 8th Division was formed from battalions from India, Egypt, Malta, Aden and South Africa). The Division landed at Le Havre in November that year and by early 1915 it was holding trenches opposite Neuve Chapelle.

The 2nd Battalion lost heavily in the early months of 1915, first through casualties suffered whilst holding the line and then in the Battle of Neuve Chapelle in March, when over 400 were killed, wounded or missing. They received new drafts of men, including some of the earliest of the Kitchener volunteers to be sent to the front. Before the Battle of Aubers Ridge, one veteran NCO said of these men: *They hadn't the training of the men of Neuve Chapelle, but they had guts and they were extraordinarily enthusiastic.* For a great many of them the assault on the Aubers Ridge on May 9th was their baptism of fire. The attack was poorly planned, there was little secrecy about the British preparations and as a result the Germans were expecting the attack. A shortage of both guns and ammunition meant that the British preliminary bombardment only lasted fifty minutes and was lacking in intensity. Nor was it very accurate, with many of the shells dropping short of their target. Throughout the bombardment the German machine guns, trained on the top of the breastworks that protected the Northamptonshire soldiers in their jumping off place, ripped the top apart. The 2nd Battalion was on the right of the 8th Division's front and given the task of breaking through the German lines in the vicinity of a position known as Rouges Bancs. When the first two companies of the 2nd Battalion went over the top at 5.30am on May 9th, they were greeted by very heavy machine gun and rifle fire and men fell in their dozens. The supporting companies fared no better. The German wire was untouched and the German soldiers were plainly visible, firing steadily over their parapets. Only a handful of the Northamptonshire men reached the German breastworks.

The survivors of the 2nd Battalion were ordered back but many had to wait until nightfall before returning. Before the action, the strength of the battalion was 20 officers and 867 other ranks; by the end of the day, 4 officers and 63 men were known to have been killed, 3 Officers and 154 men were missing; the total casualties were 426.

The Regimental History described the Battle of Aubers Ridge as a shambles and the two regular battalions as terribly mauled. Sidney was one of the men at first missing, later confirmed as killed.

Sidney's body could not be found and buried in a Commonwealth War Grave so his name is recorded on the Ploegsteert Memorial, (Panel 7). Many of those commemorated on the memorial did not die in major offensives, many of them were killed in day to day trench warfare or in small set engagements that were carried out in support of the major attacks elsewhere.

The sounding of the Last Post takes place on the first Friday of every month at 7pm at the Memorial.

The local Independent Newspaper reported on 24th July 1915: *Lance Corporal Sidney G.A. Brown, 'A' Company 8th Battalion Northamptonshire Regiment had been missing since 9th May. He had been living in Ecton where his grandmother still resided. Sidney's two sisters Mrs. S. Woods of Grafton Underwood, Kettering and Mrs. Ager of 137 Campbell St. Sarnia, Ontario, Canada had written to the paper to ask if anyone had further information about him. The paper had pages and pages of similar enquiries from relatives re: missing men.*

SAMUEL DEXTER (1891-1917)

Samuel was the son of George and Rebecca Dexter, before the war he worked as a stockman on a local farm. On Sundays he acted as a server in Ecton church, assisting Reverend Jephson. He was also a bell ringer and his name is on the plaque in the Belfry. In 1916 he married Maud Olive Blackwell from King Street, Earls Barton.

Samuel enlisted into the 6th Battalion Northamptonshire Regiment (Private 27208). A service battalion formed at Northampton in September 1914 and made up of men who had responded to the appeal by Lord Kitchener and were known as the Kitchener Volunteers. The Battalion was attached to the 18th (Eastern) Division stationed at Colchester. In November 1914 they joined the 54th Brigade. In May 1915 the Brigade went to Salisbury Plain for training before embarking, in the July, for France. As Samuel joined the Regiment in 1916 he was probably sent out with reinforcements for the Battalion.

Unfortunately all other service records for Samuel have been destroyed.

At the time he died the 6th Battalion were advancing after the Germans who were retreating to the Hindenberg Line. A patrol had reported the German evacuation of the Loupart Line and on March 18th Lieutenant Colonel R. Turner of the 6th commanded the advance guard who attacked in columns of four over ground recently held by the Germans. This continued for seven and a half miles until the village of Croisilles, which was found to be heavily defended. On the 19th of March the Battalion attacked in a line of Companies but things did not go well and the casualties were heavy.

Samuel was killed in action on 20th March 1917 aged 26, and is remembered on the Arras Memorial (Bay 7) situated about 13km from Croisilles.

The Arras Memorial commemorates almost 35,000 servicemen from the United Kingdom, South Africa and New Zealand, who have no known grave and who died in the Arras sector between the Spring and the 7th August 1918, the eve of the " Advance to Victory".

RALPH EDWIN ELSON (1897-1917)

Born in Brafield on the Green, known throughout his childhood as Ray, he lived with his grandparents James Elson and Elizabeth (nee Whitting) in High St. Ecton. In 1911, when he worked for Canon Jephson, training to become a gardener, he became closely involved with the church, acting as a server, singing in the choir and was a bell ringer, remembered on the Belfry plaque.

Ralph enlisted at Earl's Barton and served in the 10th Battalion of the Essex Regiment (Private 33938). The 10th Essex was a Kitchener Volunteer Service Battalion, formed at Warley in September 1914 as part of the 53rd Brigade, 18th (Eastern) Division. It had gone to France in July 1915 and served on the Western Front.

In August 1917, the 10th Battalion was involved in the 3rd Battle of Ypres and on 10th August 1917 they began a tour of duty in the shattered remains of the woods at the infamous Stirling Castle. (This was part of the Ypres Salient, named by the Argyll and Sutherland Highlanders, when they had set up a depot there.) There was little contact fighting during that time. *T.M.Banks and R.A.Chell in their book "With the 10th Essex in France", described this period as: it must be counted among the hardest spells of garrison duty that fell to the Battalion. Shelling had caused a good many casualties and as the 10th Essex relieved the 7th Queens, the place was described to them as: the height of everything that was unpleasant.*

One problem was caused by a German pill-box at the corner of Inverness Copse and a minor operation was planned for the morning of 12th August to deal with this. It was considered a 'one officer job'. The man who volunteered to lead two platoons from 'D' Company was Lieutenant Rex Compton, who had learnt the day before, of the death of his brother. (*Guy Compton, 8th Battalion, The Royal Sussex Regiment, who died on July 27th.*) Compton's offer was only accepted as no-one else was available. Zero hour was fixed for 4.20am on the 12th but at the last moment the attack was cancelled. This news did not reach the attacking party until 4.10am. However there was no time to stop the barrage and Compton: *either with set purpose or on the spur of a gallant impulse*; went ahead anyway. The attacking party had 150 yards to cover before they reached the pill-box. Unfortunately the British barrage had fallen behind the pill-box and with no other attacks taking place at the time; the German machine gunners were able to concentrate on Compton's party. The Divisional history states that Compton was killed and his party cut to pieces. It would seem likely that Ralph Elson was killed taking part in this desperate venture, following an officer whose judgement was apparently impaired by a sense of personal loss.

Ralph has no known grave and is commemorated on the Ypres (Menin Gate) Memorial (Panel 39) and on the same memorial are the names of Lieutenant Rex Compton and his brother 2nd Lieutenant Guy Compton.

The Ypres (Menin Gate) Memorial commemorates more than 54,000 officers and men whose graves are not known. It is one of four Belgian (Flanders) memorials to the missing in the area of the Ypres Salient. Each night the traffic is stopped at the Menin Gate at 8pm and members of the local Fire Brigade sound the Last Post in the roadway under the arches.

JOHN THOMAS GARLEY (1879-1919)

John known as Thomas, married Lillie (Lily) Eliza H. Randall of Ecton in 1900. Thomas was born in Weston Favell and worked as a plasterer. In 1901 he lived at 18 Florence Road, Northampton, with Lily, their son James, born 1900 and Lily's sister Elizabeth Randall born 1885, a dressmaker. In 1911 Thomas and Lily with their

children, Jim (10), Lilly (8), Anny (7), John (3) and George (1 month) were living in Ecton.

Thomas enlisted in the Royal Engineers (Private 304459). Unfortunately there are no surviving service records and so far a medal card hasn't come to light. It is known that he was promoted to Sergeant during his service. Thomas died on 28th January 1919, aged 40 and is commemorated with sixteen other servicemen from various regiments in Dagenham (Saints Peter and Paul cemetery) with a headstone erected by the Commonwealth War Graves Commission. There are no details about his death and he could have been a victim of the influenza which swept across the country, eventually killing more people than actually died in the war, or he could have been back in England, in hospital recovering from wounds.

There are no photographs of John Thomas Garley and no records of him or his family in Ecton after 1915.

EDGAR HERBERT HENSMAN (1885-1916)

Edgar's father, John Elson Hensman, married first of all Sophia Creamer and had two children Frederick George and Annie. After his first wife's death he married Martha also Creamer in 1883. Their only son Edgar was born in 1885.

Edgar was a member of the church choir. He was studious and hard-working at school and by 1901 had become a Pupil Teacher. According to the 1911 census, he had left Ecton and was living as a boarder with William Chapman and his family at 125, Waddon New Road, Croydon, Surrey and was working as a fully qualified teacher.

In 1914 he enlisted (Private P.S.1195, the P.S. indicating Public Schools Battalion), at Kempton Park, Middlesex with the Duke of Cambridge's Own Middlesex Regiment, 16th (Service) Battalion. The 16th Battalion was formed in London on 1st September 1914 by Lieutenant Colonel J.J. MacKay and first moved to Kempton Park Racecourse. In July 1915 the Battalion moved on to Clipstone Camp, Nottinghamshire. It was attached to the 100th Brigade 33rd Division, embarking for France in November 1915.

On 17th November 1915 the Battalion landed in Boulogne from where they marched to the town of Bethune. There they took over a section of the line at Annequin North, just to the east of Bethune, alternating tours of duty in the trenches and relaxation in billets at Bethune.

During incidents in the trenches in their first tour, which lasted from 4th to 14th January 1916, they had one officer and eleven other ranks killed and twenty four other ranks wounded. Their second tour commenced on 27th January and was to last until 2nd February. On 28th January the front line and support trenches were heavily bombarded with two officers and two other ranks killed and fifteen other ranks wounded. At 11am on 29th January the Commanding Officer received a verbal order from the General Officer Commanding the 100th Brigade, to make a bombing attack on the German line at an area named Mad Point. At 9pm that night, three patrols went out to reconnoitre returning at 1am on the 30th having lost one officer and one other rank killed, one other rank wounded and one officer missing believed killed. The bombing attack was subsequently cancelled.

At some point during the second tour of the trenches made by the 16th Battalion, Edgar Hensman was wounded, dying of his wounds on 31st January. At the time of his death Edgar had been promoted to Lance Sergeant (1195).

He is buried in Cambrin Churchyard Extension (L.3). The proximity of his resting place to the front line suggests he died before there was time to evacuate him further back and may point to his being wounded in the ill-fated reconnaissance on the night of 29th/30th January. Otherwise, it would seem likely he was wounded by shellfire on the 28th January 1916.

The Churchyard Extension contains 1,211 Commonwealth burials from the First World War, 8 unidentified. Also the graves of 98 French, 1 Belgian and 3 German servicemen.

HORACE ALFRED HENSMAN (1896-1916)

In 1911 Horace, his two brothers and his parents, Alfred and Eleanor, were living in the Three Horseshoes public house in High Street, Ecton. Later they moved to Leicester to keep the Old Crown Inn in Shearsby and then to the Chandlers Arms also in Shearsby.

Whilst in Ecton the older boys sang in the church choir and Horace was one of the bell ringers on the plaque in the Belfry. He left school at 14 and became a clerk in the office of a shoe manufacturer.

After the family had moved to Shearsby, Horace was employed on the staff at St. Andrews Hospital in Northampton. He enlisted on 1st September 1914 into the 7th Bedfordshire Regiment (Private 13015). The Battalion was a Kitchener Volunteer Battalion and had been formed at Guildford in September 1914 and attached to the 54th Brigade, 18th (Eastern) Division. In July 1915 the Brigade sailed to France and landed at Boulogne.

The 7th Bedfordshire Regiment spent a year in the trenches opposite Fricourt, near Carnoy, in the Somme sector of the front. It was involved in the opening day of the Battle of the Somme, 1st July 1916, attacking German positions close to Fricourt. It was on this day that Horace was killed.

Horace was in the signallers section of 'A' Company, which was in support of the first wave of infantry attacks and passed through the British wire at 7.40am ten minutes after the start of the first attack. As the Company moved forward they faced a series of barrages of shrapnel plus machine gun fire. By the time they reached Pommiers Redoubt, which had been taken, they had passed through three German barrages and although it is not clear at which point Horace was mortally wounded, half the Company's losses occurred when they were passing through the British wire.

Horace is buried in Dantzig Alley British Cemetery at Mametz, (III.D.5), a little to the west of where his Battalion was in action. The Cemetery was used by both field ambulances and fighting units. After the front was regained in August 1918 a few graves were added and at the Armistice the cemetery consisted of 183 graves brought in from battlefields and from smaller burial grounds. Today it contains 2,053 burials and commemorations. 518 of which are unidentified.

The Northampton Independent on 27th January 1917 reports:
Reported wounded and missing after an engagement on July 1st, Private Horace Alfred Hensman of the Bedfords, is now officially stated to have been killed on that date. Nineteen years of age, the son of Mr. and Mrs.A.Hensman of Shearsby, Rugby and formerly of Ecton. He enlisted on September 1st 1914 and went to France in the following July. Prior to enlisting he was employed on the staff of St.Andrew's Hospital. In a letter to the bereaved parents his Captain writes:-"He was a splendid lad, and one whom I could always trust. By his courage and devotion to duty at all times he earned the regard of the whole battalion, and we deeply feel his death". A younger brother is serving with the Rifle Brigade.

HARRY LIONEL JOHNSON (1883-1918)

One of the six sons of Charles and Rachel Johnson of Ecton, Harry married Lilian Taylor on 23rd April 1906 in Bradford, Yorkshire. They emigrated to Canada aboard the Empress of Ireland in 1911 with their daughter Eva aged 3. Their son Charles had been born in Bradford in 1906 and sadly died the same year. In 1912 they had a third child Alice, born in Hamilton, Ontario, Canada. The family lived at 26, Severn Street, Hamilton, where Harry worked as a Streetcar Conductor until he enlisted with the Canadian Expeditionary Force on 1st March 1916.

Enlisting in the 75th Battalion Canadian Infantry (Central Ontario Regiment, Private 690362), Harry gave his religion as Non-Conformist. He was five feet four inches tall with a ruddy complexion, hazel eyes and brown hair, with scars on the bridge of his nose and the back of his right hand.

At the end of August 1918 the Canadian Divisions of General Julian Byng's Third Army started their push from the edge of Arras. The first major line of defence was the Droquort/Queant line which lay astride the Arras/Cambrai Road, crossing the Mont Dury Rise. The Canadian Corps took the villages of Vis-En-Artois and Haucourt on 27th August 1918, which, together with the capture of Peronne by the Australians, forced Ludendorff to withdraw to the Sensee and the Canal du Nord on the night of the 2nd September. From here the Canadians pursued the Germans until they reached the Hindenburg

Line on the Canal du Nord. Harry was killed in the fighting in the area on 2nd September 1918.

He is buried in the Vis-en-Artois British Cemetery, Haucourt. (Plot II. Row B. Grave 26). His name is on page 437 of the First World War Book of Remembrance in Canada.

Burials were made in the cemetery from August 1918; it is situated on the road from Arras to Cambrai. The cemetery was used by the fighting units and field ambulances until the middle of October 1918. Originally it contained 430 graves of which 297 were Canadian. These are in plots I and II, the cemetery was later increased and today it contains 2,369 burials and commemorations of the First World War. 1,458 are unidentified.

Harry's daughters Eva Robinson and Alice Stokes and his grandsons were living in Hamilton, Ontario, Canada.

ERNEST JAMES JOLLEY (1894-1918)

Ernest was the eldest son of Thomas Kemp Jolley and his wife Sarah (nee Hyde). Thomas Kemp worked as a general labourer on the Ecton Estate and by 1911 Ernest was working as a domestic groom for the Sotheby family and lived at The Stables, Ecton House.

Ernest enlisted in the Norfolk Regiment (Private 23684) and at the time of his death he was serving with the 1st Battalion Bedfordshire Regiment as Lance Corporal (33345), attached to the 15th Brigade, 5th Division. His service records have not survived.

In 1916 the 1st Battalion Bedfordshires were involved in several phases of the Battle of the Somme, namely the attacks on High Wood and Longueval in July, also the Battle of Guillemont and the Battle of Flers-Courcelette in September. In 1917 they were involved in the Battle of Arras, specifically at the attack on La Coulotte in April and the Third Battle of the Scarpe in May. In June they were involved in the capture of Oppy Wood and Passchendaele (Third Battle of Ypres). As well as the Third Battle of Ypres they took part in the battles of Broodseinde and Poelcapelle in October, whilst in November 1917 they were moved to Italy to help stabilise the front there.

On 3rd April 1918 they prepared to entrain from Italy back to the Western Front in response to the German Spring Offensives. The trains arrived in Frevent and the men marched to Neuvillette where they were billeted. The battalions were in readiness to move where needed at very short notice. They fought in the Battle of the Lys during the defence of the Nieppe Forest in the Battle of Hazebrouck.

In July whilst in the trenches they suffered from heavy shelling and the Battalion War Diary reports that one man was wounded on 12th July 1918. Ernest Jolley could have been this man, as no-one else is reported wounded until after he had died from his wounds on 16th July 1918.

He is buried in Mount Huon Military Cemetery, Le Treport. (V.M. 4B).

Le Treport was an important hospital centre and by July 1916 the town contained three general hospitals, a Convalescent Depot and a British Red Cross Hospital. As the original cemetery at Le Treport filled it became necessary to use the new site at Mount Huon. In this cemetery are 2,128 Commonwealth burials of the First World War, 7 from the Second and also more than 200 German war graves.

FREDERICK WILLIAM JOLLEY (1893-1918)

Frederick, a cousin of Ernest James Jolley had lived with his grandparents George and Hannah, his mother Lizzie Jolley having died in 1903.

Frederick joined the Northamptonshire Regiment (Private 23024) on 15th November 1915 and was sent to the Army Reserve until he was mobilised into the 3rd Battalion on 9th February 1916. He was twenty three years and five months of age and five feet seven inches in height. Army life obviously suited him, as on a medical history form one month after he enlisted his height had increased to five feet nine inches. On the 11th February 1916 he was posted to the 1/12 Battalion London Regiment (Private 7927) and later to the 23rd Battalion London Regiment (Private 718059). Amongst his service records is a note from the Northamptonshire Regiment stating that Frederick was a first class shot.

He embarked from England on 26th June 1916 for Le Havre and served in France until, he died on 8th April 1918, from gunshot wounds in the chest received during an attack on 5th April.

It was learned that a German attack was expected on the 47th Division's positions and the bombardment began at 6.30am. It became more intense and was accompanied by an infantry assault. The German troops were attacking through the heavy clouds of gas and smoke. This was part of a more general attack along the British

IV Corps front. The attack came from the south-east with the aim of taking Bouzincourt and Mesnil. It fell first on the 142nd Brigade (47th Division) at 7.20am. The Germans were met with sustained rifle, Lewis-gun and artillery fire but succeeded in breaking the line of the Brigade in Aveluy Wood between the two battalions positioned there. One company of the 23rd Battalion London Regiment was almost wiped out after desperate resistance. By 6pm the incessant shelling died down and although failing to regain the original British line, a continuous line of defence had been established along the slope above the western edge of Aveluy Wood. Aveluy Wood was part of the 1916 Somme battlefield, which was behind the British Line of 1st July 1916. It was situated on the west bank of the River Ancre about 3 kilometres north of the town of Albert.

Frederick's personal effects were returned to his Grandfather, George Jolley, High St. Ecton, on July 30th 1918. Namely: *Coins, Pipe, Pocket Book, Religious Book, Cigarette Case, Tobacco Box, Scissors, Wrist Watch (broken), Strap, Protector, Purse.*

A list of Relatives of the Deceased was required by the War Record Office and this was witnessed by the Baptist Minister in Ecton, John Field. Frederick's closest relatives were: George Jolly, Grandfather, Henry Jolly (53) and Charles Jolly (41) both of Ecton also Ellen Waples (51) of Earls Barton.

Frederick is buried in Boulogne Eastern Cemetery (VIII.1.183). The cemetery is a large civil cemetery. The Commonwealth War Graves plot is located on the western edge of the southern section of the cemetery. The headstones are laid flat due to the sandy soil. Boulogne and Wimereux formed one of the chief hospital areas. The cemetery contains 5,577 burials.

HERBERT KNIGHT (1887-1917)

*The son of Rowlat Knight and Elizabeth (nee Luck), who lived in
Little Billing, Northamptonshire.*

*Herbert was a local milkman. In 1913 he married Annie Jordan
Penn a dressmaker born in Ecton in 1876. Herbert and Annie had a
daughter Eva born 1ˢᵗ November 1914. (Eva married Leslie Warren
and she is buried in Ecton Churchyard). There is a marble plaque to
Herbert on the wall of the church: Sacred to the memory of my dear
husband Herbert Knight, R.W.S. Regt. killed in action in France
September 22 1917 aged 30 years. "Therefore is he before the
throne of God."*

Herbert enlisted in the Queen's (Royal West Surrey) Regiment
(Private G/13735). The Queen's was sometimes known as the
Mutton Lancers after their Lamb and Flag cap badge. Herbert was
killed in action on 22ⁿᵈ September 1917 whilst serving with the 10ᵗʰ
Battalion in France. The 10ᵗʰ (Service) Battalion was raised with
mainly Kitchener Volunteers by the Mayor and Borough of
Battersea in June 1915, it joined the 124ᵗʰ Brigade, 41ˢᵗ Division.
Just before leaving England in April, they were inspected by King
George V and Field Marshal Lord French, whilst they were in the
Stanhope Lines, Aldershot. In May 1916 the Division landed at Le
Havre.

In 1916 the 41st Division suffered huge losses at Fleurs and were reformed in 1917 when they moved to Belgium and took part in the opening stages of the Battle of the Menin Road, one of the subsidiary battles that made up the Third Battle of Ypres. The 10th Battalion of The Queen's were one of the Division's attacking battalions and took their objectives despite heavy machine gun fire. During the evening of 20th September they beat off repeated German counter attacks. Over the following two days they held onto their gains despite continued shelling and a further German counter attack. On 22nd the positions were shelled during the day and there was great difficulty in getting in touch with various posts owing to snipers and machine gun fire. The men suffered from a lack of sufficient food and water. At some point on the 22nd Herbert Knight was killed, although whether this was a result of shelling, sniping or machine gun fire is not known. This battle was not trench warfare and Herbert would have probably died in one of the isolated posts, often no more than shell holes, amidst the devastated landscape that constituted the Ypres Salient in 1917.

Herbert is buried in Tyne Cot Cemetery, (LV. A. 6) in September 1917 the position of the cemetery was in German hands, so his body must have been moved there after the war from a smaller plot. The vast concentration of bodies turned Tyne Cot into the biggest British War Cemetery in the world.

The Northamptonshire Independent reported: *that after being at the front for twelve months Private H. Knight of the Queens Own Royal West Surrey Regiment was reported killed in action between 20th and 22nd September. The deceased, who was 30 years old, was the husband of Mrs. Knight of Ecton and youngest son of Mrs. R. Knight of Little Billing. He enlisted in May 1916 and had been working for Messrs. Knight and Glen of Little Billing.*

WILLIAM MABBUTT (1886-1917)

In 1908 William, the son of Ambrose and Sarah Mabbutt, married Daisy May, she already had a daughter, Nelly May aged 5. William and Daisy had a son William Arthur born in Mears Ashby in 1909 and by 1911 they were living in Ecton. William sang in the church choir and the comment in the Ecton War Book is that he was a good bass singer and was 38 when he was killed.

William enlisted in the Northamptonshire Regiment (Private 4292) and was transferred to the 8th Battalion of the Leicestershire Regiment, (Private 3326). During his service with them he was promoted to Acting Corporal. The 8th Battalion of the Leicester Regiment had been formed in September 1914, from the third new army of Kitchener Volunteers (K3). The 8th Battalion was a service battalion attached to the 21st Division part of the 110th Brigade, which landed in France on the 7th July 1916.

William Mabbutt died in the later stages of the Battle of Polygon Wood, one of the subsidiary battles of the Third Battle of Ypres. The fighting around Polygon Wood had started with a major British offensive on 26th September. By the time the 110th Brigade went into the battle, Polygon Wood or the remains of it, had been captured by Australian forces.

On the night of 30th September, the Leicester Regiment moved forward along duck-board tracks to take over the newly won positions outside the wood. The 8th and 9th Battalions occupied the Brigade frontage, with the 6th and 7th Battalions in reserve. Early in the morning of October 1st the Germans launched a strong counter-attack aimed at regaining their lost positions. The attack was preceded by a heavy artillery barrage, which had begun at 4.40am. The German artillery also fired smoke shells aimed at concealing the build up of their infantry. The brunt of the attack fell on the 8th Battalion of the Leicester Regiment, who were forced back as were the 9th Battalion. However, a defensive line was re-established and the German attack held in check. A further German counter-attack was made at dusk but this was dispersed by the British artillery. German shelling continued during the night but the battle was petering out and is considered to have ended on 3rd October. The casualties suffered by the 8th and 9th Battalions were such that the decision was taken on 4th October to amalgamate the two battalions until such time as each could be brought up to strength.

William Mabbutt was killed in action on 2nd October, after the hardest fighting around Polygon Wood had finished.
His body was recovered and now lies in Hooge Crater Cemetery (XI. L. 8).

This is one of the largest cemeteries in the Ypres Salient, with nearly 6,000 men buried there. However, all but 76 of these were brought to the cemetery after the war, as some of the smaller cemeteries in the area were closed and their dead concentrated at Hooge Crater. William Mabbutt's original resting place was almost certainly elsewhere.

THOMAS GORDON PARK (1899-1918)

Thomas was the son of Thomas and Clara (nee Chapman) who married in 1889, he was born in Northampton, his father Thomas a slater, was born in Manchester and his mother, Clara in Northampton. Thomas had an elder sister, Florence born in Blackpool.

In 1891 Thomas and Clara were living in 16, Grosvenor St., Layton-with-Warbreck, Blackpool, however, they later moved to Harnall Lane, Coventry, where Thomas died in 1899 and is buried in the London Road Cemetery. After his death Clara moved to 115 Stanley Road, Dallington, Northampton. By 1901 she was working as a Housekeeper. In 1903 Clara married her second husband William Timms and in 1911 they were living at Rectory Farm, Ecton. Clara became step mother to Bertie and Percy Timms who also fought in the war. Whilst living in the village Thomas sang in the church choir and was one of the bell ringers remembered on the plaque in the Belfry. He worked for the Sotheby Family. (Clara died in November 1912 and she is buried in London Road Cemetery, Coventry, with her first husband).

Thomas entered the Royal Naval Volunteer Reserve on 31st July 1917 (Able Seaman R/5654). He was in the draft for the British Expeditionary Force on 2nd April 1918 and joined the Hawke Battalion, one of the Royal Naval Division Battalions.

The Royal Naval Division (RND) had been formed in 1914 from a surplus of between 20,000 and 30,000 men who had volunteered for the RND. The men, who could not be placed in service on a warship were used to create two Naval Brigades and a Brigade of Marines. So despite joining the navy Thomas never fought at sea.

After taking part in the Gallipoli campaign, the RND passed from the control of the Admiralty to that of the War Office and was re-designated the 63rd (Royal Naval) Division and served the rest of the war on the Western Front. Throughout the war members of the RND retained their naval rank.

In the summer of 1918, the RND was experiencing a period of training and re-organisation, following the defensive battles of the spring, in which Thomas Park had presumably taken part. Between 20th and 23rd of August they were involved in the fighting that became known as the Battle of Albert, part of the major Allied counter-offensive launched against the Germans in the summer of 1918. The offensive was renewed on 24th August, with the RND being ordered forward to attack the village of Grevillers, just to the west of the ruined town of Bapaume. However, because of the uncertainty regarding both the strength and location of German forces, the Hawke Battalion started their advance at 6am. On the left the Companies moved forward without much opposition and reached high ground east of the village of Thilloy. On the right the Companies suffered grievous losses, as did Companies from the Hood Battalion of the RND. The Commanders of both the Hawke and Hood Battalions were amongst those killed as their Battalions attacked German trench systems facing the southwest corner of Loupart Wood. About noon the German defenders fell back and the RND's advance resumed. Although its objectives were not all reached, Bapaume was effectively isolated and was taken a few days later.

Thomas Park was reported missing, assumed killed in action, on 25th August. He has no known grave and is commemorated on the Vis-en-Artois Memorial (MR16). He was 19 years old at the time of his death.

The memorial consists of a screen in three parts and bears the names of over 9,000 men from Great Britain, Ireland and South Africa who died from 8th August to the date of the Armistice in the area.

As well as informing his step-father of his death, the RND also informed Thomas' guardian, his mother's brother, Mr.E.Chapman, 20, Lightwoods Hill, Warley, Lancashire.

LIONEL FREDERICK SOUTHWELL SOTHEBY (1895-1915)

The eldest son of William and Margaret Southwell Sotheby, Lionel followed his father to Eton where he joined the Eton College Officers Training Course (Army). He left school in 1913, to pursue a career in the business world and spent a number of months studying German, at the Institute Tilly in Berlin, before returning to England July 1914.

When Lionel joined the Argyll and Sutherland Highlanders, on 15th August 1914, on the outbreak of war, he was twenty. Starting army life as a Subaltern in A Company, No.2 Platoon in the 4th Battalion he arrived at Crown Hill Hutments, Devonport, for training and after six weeks left for Newcastle, his Company patrolling a section of the Sunderland North Sea coast.

He embarked for France on 2nd January 1915, disembarking at Le Havre and from there was posted to No.9 Camp, No.1 Infantry Base Depot near Harfleur. Here he was transferred to the 2nd Battalion the Black Watch at Bethune. Upon arrival in Bethune he was attached to the 1st Battalion the Black Watch, in 1st Division, 1st Corps. They had been in France since mid August 1914 fighting at Mons, the Marne, the Aisne and first Battle of Ypres and also on the front lines at Festubert throughout the winter. *A Seaforth officer said of the Black Watch that: "It was as good as signing your death warrant to join them, as they were practically in all the worse fighting". (Page 5 of Donald Richter's book Lionel Sotheby's Great War, his letters and diary).*

When on leave, Lionel was able to visit his father, William, who had volunteered as a driver for the Red Cross, using his own car and was in Northern France.

With the 1st Battalion Lionel saw a great deal of action both in support roles and in opposing a German counter attack at the Battle of Neuve Chapelle in March 1915, again in the Battle of Aubers Ridge on 9th May. Following the losses incurred by the 1st Battalion at Aubers Ridge they moved back to Bethune and Beuvry for reorganisation and replacement manpower. On the evening of 10th June they relieved the 2nd Battalion Royal Munster Fusiliers at Cuinchy on the south side of La Basse Canal. In July Lionel was transferred back to the 2nd Battalion the Black Watch and was with them on 24th August in the trenches opposite Aubers Ridge. At this time the army were preparing for the autumn offensive at Loos together with the French attack at Champagne.

Lionel was described as brave, resilient, cheerful, enduring rain, lice, discomfort, illness and narrow escapes from death. He knew he might be killed. He wrote in his diary in March 1915 that as a platoon commander it was his duty: "to encourage his men and expose himself more than anyone. For an attack he has to be in the front and first in everything "(Richter).

On 25th September 1915 the battle of Loos began. The Bareilly and Garhwal Brigades were to lead as a feint attack on the Moulin du Pietre. In the front lines were the 2nd Black Watch and the 69th Punjabis and a Territorial unit also of the Black Watch. Lionel's battalion in the leading wave were engulfed in drifting gas which had been released under the German trenches but a gust of wind had turned the gas cloud back onto the British lines. In the chaos of the battle on the Moulin the 2nd Black Watch lost 363 including 91 killed and 271 wounded. Amongst the bodies missing and never recovered was that of 2nd Lieutenant Sotheby aged 21. *In an account, sent by Major Wauchope, Lionel's battalion commander, to his parents he reported: "He was wounded and continued leading his men until a grenade struck him and killed him."*

Whether the Major actually witnessed the death or sent this account to console the family is not known.

Lionel's name is on the Addenda panel of the Loos Memorial. The Memorial forms the sides and back of the Dud Corner Cemetery, standing on the site of a German strong point, the Lens Road Redoubt, which was captured by the 15th (Scottish) Division on the first day of the battle.

He is also remembered on the Shrine in Ecton and in St. Mary's Church, Gillingham, Kent, where his uncle was Rector, also on the War Memorial at Dwyran, Methodist Welsh Church near his family's estate.

In March 1920 his father W.E.Sotheby applied for the 1914-15 Star and other medals due to his son.

On the bottom of his medal card is the note M.I.D. LG1-1-16 page 55 (London Gazette, 1st January 1916, page 55). Lionel received a posthumous Mention in Despatches, Sir John French commending him for his gallant and distinguished service in the field. (*Lionel's war diary and letters home have been edited by Donald C. Richter "Lionel Sotheby's Great War"*)

GEOFFREY WILLIAM STOPFORD-SACKVILLE
(1893-1915)

Geoffrey was born *on 22nd May 1893 at South Raglan Barracks Devonport, Devon, the son of Colonel Lionel Richard Stopford-Sackville and Constance Evelyn (nee Gosling). He was educated at St. Peters Court, Broadstairs, Osborn School and Dartmouth Royal Naval College. He served on three ships, the St. Vincent, as a midshipman from 15th May 1911 to 14th January 1912, the Cornwallis 15th January 1912 to 20th September 1913 and finally the Invincible from 30th September to 31st December 1913.*

In Portsmouth following a three month course in H.M.Ships, *Victory, Excellent* and *Dryad,* during which he obtained a First Class Seamanship Certificate, Geoffrey was promoted to Sub-Lieutenant on 30th May 1914 and posted to the HMS *Hampshire*. He never served in her, arriving in Hong Kong to join the *Hampshire* he and the rest of the crew, were sent to a Britomart Class Gunboat. On the outbreak of war 5th August 1914 they were all transferred to HMS, River Class Destroyer *Ribble* launched in 1905. They assisted in the Gallipoli landings transporting part of the Australian 12th Battalion just north of a promontory called Ari Burnu and close to what is now known as Anzac Cove.

The destroyer had initially towed six lifeboats close into the shore so that troops from the *Ribble* could be transferred and then the lifeboats were to be towed onto the shore by smaller steamboats. On 25th April the boats were returning from towing the first wave of troops to shore when, before Commander Ralph Wilkinson, Captain of HMS *Ribble*, could release the next wave of troops, the Turkish defenders opened fire from the cliffs at a range of about 300 yards. Immediately two of the destroyer's crew were killed and another 15 wounded. One of those hit was Geoffrey. He was severely wounded and died in the Bombay Relief Fund Hospital, Alexandria aged 22.

His Company Commander R.Wilkinson wrote: "Geoffrey was struck in the forehead, standing aft and superintending the disembarkation of soldiers, cheering them up in his quiet manly way. He was always keen to go into action and to be doing something".

Geoffrey Stopford-Sackville is buried in Alexandria (Chatby) Military and War Memorial Cemetery (Q. 470). Chatby is a district on the eastern side of the city of Alexandria. This was originally the Garrison cemetery and was used for burials until April 1916 when a new cemetery was opened at Hadra. Some graves were brought into Chatby after the war from other burial grounds in the area. There are 2,259 First World War burials in the cemetery.

Alexandria became a camp and hospital centre for Commonwealth and French troops. It was used by hospital ships and troop transports bringing reinforcements and carrying the sick and wounded.

BERTIE TIMMS (1893-1916)

The son of William and Francis (nee Norris) Timms, Bertie was born in Luddington, Northamptonshire. His parents' families came from Warwickshire. Bertie's father, William, was working as a Farm Bailiff and the family were living at Pentelows Farmhouse, Luddington-in-the-Brook when Bertie was born. His mother, Francis, died when he was eight. In 1903 his father married Clara Park, widowed mother of Thomas Gordon Park, who is also commemorated on the Shrine.

Bertie worked as a page in a Dining Saloon in Harlesden, Middlesex and aged 22 enlisted on 25th November 1915 at Mill Hill into the Duke of Cambridge's Own (Middlesex Regiment) 23rd (Service) 2nd (Football) Battalion (Private F/3222, the *"F"* in his service number indicating *Footballer).* This Battalion was formed in London in June 1915 by W. Joynson Hicks M.P. It moved to Cranleigh in Surrey and from there in November 1915, to Aldershot where they were attached to the 123rd Brigade, 41st Division. Bertie was mobilized on 9th February 1916 and the Regiment left for France in May 1916.

After a brief induction into trench warfare upon arrival in France, the 23rd Battalion then moved on to the Somme area, taking part in the Battle of the Somme which had begun on 1st July 1916. Further training behind the line was followed by a move to the Delville Wood sector of the front on 10th September. The 23rd Middlesex worked on the preparations being made for a major British attack to be launched on 15th September, helping to push trenches out towards the village of Flers, thus providing jumping off positions for the attack. They were subject to heavy enemy shelling and suffered nearly 50 casualties. After a short respite behind the line they moved forward to assembly positions on the night of 14th/15th September.

The major offensive which started on September 15th was to last until September 22nd, known as the Battle of Flers-Courcelette and often remembered as the first occasion on which tanks were used in battle. The 123rd Brigade, which included the 23rd Middlesex, was in reserve on 15th September and moved forward nearly four hours after the start of the battle to help consolidate the gains made following the capture of Flers. The Battalion changed position more than once during the course of the day, subjected to enemy shelling and suffering casualties throughout. Most of the following day the Battalion found itself hanging onto a position east of Flers and exposed to heavy shell fire, sweeping across the position. When the Battalion was withdrawn in the evening of September 26[th]it had suffered nearly 200 casualties.

According to his service record Bertie received a gun shot wound in his side whilst in action on 29th September 1916 and was treated in a Field hospital. He was treated again on 13th October and was admitted to the General Hospital at Rouen on October 22nd. By the 27th he was reported as seriously ill and he died in hospital on that day. Rouen was a major hospital centre which received many casualties from the Battle of the Somme, of which Flers-Courcelette was a subsidiary battle.

Bertie was 23 and is buried in the St. Sever Cemetery, Rouen (B23.58). This is within a communal cemetery on the eastern edge of the southern Rouen suburbs and contains 3,082 burials plus one French and one non war service burial.

HARRY EDWARD TIPLER (1884-1916)

Harry was the only son of Edward and his wife Lucy, he was born in Ecton, where in 1901 he was working as a carpenter's apprentice. According to the 1911 census he had moved to Chesterfield in Derbyshire, working as a platelayer for the Midland Railway. Harry never married.

From Derbyshire, age 30, Harry went to London and enlisted in the 111th Railway Company, Royal Engineers (Sapper 55357). In February 1915 the Company arrived in France, where in Rouen in July 1916 Harry sadly died as a result of a bathing accident.

At the ensuing Court of Inquiry, Sapper Butler, who was with Harry Tipler at the time of his death, reported that the two men had come off guard duty and decided to bathe in a nearby ballast pit. Neither of the men could swim and Sapper Butler was standing up to his arm pits in water about four yards from the bank washing, when after five minutes Sapper Tipler commenced to struggle and nearly pulled him under. Then Sapper Tipler disappeared. Sapper Butler ran back to the camp to get help and met Captain E.A. Wilson outside the company's blacksmith shop.

Captain E. A. Wilson R.E. stated at the Court of Inquiry that just about 2.30pm he was outside the blacksmith's shop of his Company when he met Sapper Butler, partially dressed, running towards the living quarters and upon seeing him Sapper Butler told him Sapper Tipler had been drowned in the ballast pit. Captain Wilson instructed him to bring a rope and went himself to the ballast pit with Sergeant Jollands. Then he sent for Corporal Thorpe who understood artificial respiration, to join them as quickly as possible. Captain Wilson was on the scene of the accident within five minutes of being informed of it. He reported that when he arrived at the scene a French lad and Sappers Bailey and Avery were there trying to find the body with a boat hook. The two Sappers undressed and got into the water, Sappers Cole, Fallows and Lowington, all good swimmers, turned up and dived for the body but were unable to find it. Private Hope was sent to fetch some grapplers. Then the Captain handed over the dragging operations to Lieutenant Phillips. Captain Wilson was present again when the body was finally recovered at 6.20pm. All the Sappers who were present at the scene reported to the subsequent Court of Inquiry and Captain Wilson added that a medical orderly, capable of rendering all necessary medical assistance to the partially drowned, was in attendance from the Medical Aid Post near the Transporter Bridge.

The Court of Inquiry into his death came to the conclusion: *"That Sapper Tipler met his death accidentally, by drowning, and that no blame is attached to any person".*
He is buried in the Bois Guillaume Communal Cemetery (11 A. 4) which contains 320 burials with an extension containing 360 burials.

In Ecton Churchyard there is a headstone: In Loving memory of Lucy the beloved wife of Edward Tipler who died 20th Jan. 1920 aged 69 years. Also their only son Sapper Harry Edward Tippler who was accidently drowned at Rouen, France 8th July 1916 aged 31 years, interred in Boisguillaine Cemetery, Rouen. Also Edward the beloved husband of Lucy Tipler who died July 1930 aged 75 years.

ANDREW WOOD (1885-1916)

Andrew Wood was the one person named on the Shrine that no-one in Ecton in recent times could recall. After months of hard searching I finally discovered him. His name is on the shrine as Andrew Wood and no mention is made of him on the Roll of Honour or in the Ecton War Book. It seemed an impossible task to find anything out about him. It didn't help that on the Medal Record Cards he was listed as Albert. However I eventually found him on the Commonwealth War Graves internet site, listed as A Wood, with his personal details given as: Son of Stephen Wood of 14, Grafton Underwood, Kettering, Northants.

My searching for Andrew had initiated my researching the other seventeen men on the Shrine and by a lucky chance I had already researched Sidney George Albert Brown. He was recorded on the Commonwealth War Graves as the son of Mrs. Sarah Ann Wood of

14, Grafton Underwood, Kettering, Northants. So I knew where to look for a connection. By the time I had found this out I was so engrossed in the men from the village who had fought, that I decided to try and find as much out as I could about all of them and hence to the writing of this book.

Knowing that Sidney was the stepson of Stephen Wood, from checking census records, it was possible to find Andrew with his father prior to his father's marriage to Sarah Ann Brown.

Andrew was step-brother to Sidney Brown. Sarah Brown brought three children to her second marriage and Stephen had two sons and a daughter. Stephen and Sarah eventually had four more daughters.

Andrew enlisted in 2nd Battalion Queen's Own, Royal West Surrey Regiment (L/8665), who were in South Africa at the outbreak of the First World War and sailed from Cape Town on 27th August 1914. They landed at Southampton on 19th September and went to Lyndhurst in Hampshire where they were attached to the 22nd Brigade, as part of the 7th Division. This was formed from regular army units from around the British Empire. By October 1914 the Brigade had landed at Zeebrugge. Here they were ordered to support Antwerp but were too late, so they seized and held important bridges to facilitate the retreat of the Belgian Army.

The 7th Division were the first British Troops to entrench in front of Ypres and here it suffered great losses in the First Battle of Ypres, 14th October 1914.

In 1915 the Division was involved in the Battles of: Neuve Chapelle, Aubers Ridge, Festubert, Givenchy (2nd battle) and Loos. Where it suffered from the British gas not moving away from the lines and consequently were badly cut up by German guns and artillery. In 1916 they were fighting on the Somme and involved in the Battles of Albert, High Wood, Delville Wood and Guillemont. This last action on 3rd September 1916, was possibly the final battle Andrew Wood was involved in. Unfortunately his service records are missing and his medal card just states baldly that he was dead.

He is remembered on the screen in Kensal Green (All Souls) Cemetery (213. 6. 9). There are 473 burials from the First World War and a screen wall which records the names of casualties. Andrew is remembered on the right hand side of the screen wall around the Cross of Remembrance.

There are no photographs of Andrew or any record of his living in Ecton.

PART II
THE MEN WHO CAME HOME

These men are listed in alphabetical order and are the men in the Ecton War Book and on the Roll of Honour.

Such information as I was able to find about their families and connection to Ecton is also included.

THOMAS FRANK BARRICK (1884-1939)

Born in 1884 Thomas Frank, known as Frank, was the second eldest of the nine children of John and Catherine (nee White) of Little Houghton. Frank and his elder brother William Alfred moved to Ecton to work. William, a waggoner, worked and lived at Irrigation Farm and Frank lived in Back Street and worked as a farm labourer. Frank married Ethel Daisy Aldridge in 1908, they had five children: Ethel May Irene (1909-2000), Percy Cyril Alfred (1910-1913), Bertha Catherine (1912-1996), Ida Lillian (1914-1986) and Edith Mary Pamela (1915-2001). According to the Ecton War Book, Frank enlisted into the Royal Army Medical Corps. He would have been 31 in 1914 and the book doesn't give the date when he enlisted. There is no surviving medal card or service recorded and the book states he was discharged in 1916. He returned to live with his family in Back Lane, Ecton his children attending the village school.

Frank died on 18th September 1939 age 56 and Ethel Daisy on 6th July 1980, they are buried in Ecton Churchyard.

WALTER DALZIEL BORROWDALE (1877-1943)

Walter Dalzel Borrowdale was born on the 15th July 1877, in Romford, Essex. One of the ten children of Walter, a Commercial Traveller in Drapery, and his wife Clara Sophia (nee Walker). His Grandfather John Willis Borrowdale was a Solicitors General Clerk.

In 1901 Walter was serving as a Stoker on H.M.S Pembroke, at the end of his tour of duty he was discharged. According to the 1911 census he was lodging in Northampton with Henry Groom and working as a caretaker for the General Post Office. In 1912 he married Emma Elizabeth Barth in Fulham. She was the daughter of Theodore William Barth who was a Professor of Singing. After their marriage they moved to Ecton.

Walter re-joined the Royal Navy at the outbreak of the war. In the baptism record of his daughter Emma in 1915 he is described as a leading stoker on H.M.S. Brilliant. According to the 1918 Absent Voters List for Ecton, Walter served on H.M.S. Wallington (Stoker M 288732) Royal Navy.

The family were recorded living in Ecton until 1921. In March 1924 Walter, Emma and their children, Ronald Walter (11) and Eileen C. (9) emigrated to Australia aboard the "Hudson Bay", a ship of the Australian Commonwealth Line. They landed at Brisbane, where they settled. According to the 1936 Australian Electoral Roll they were at 74 Enggoera Terrace, Red Hill and Walter's occupation was given as a waterside worker. Walter died in January 1943.

WILLIAM GEORGE BRAWN (1896-1975)

Born in 1896 in Abington, Northampton, William was the son of George Brawn, an Agricultural Labourer and Annie Elizabeth (nee Flint). In 1901 the family were living in Weston Favell. George died early in the marriage and in 1907 Annie Elizabeth married Thomas Attwell. They are listed in the 1911 census as living in High Street, Ecton with William 15 and their own two sons Albert John 3 and Thomas James 1.
For three years before the war William worked for Mrs. Callis at West Lodge, Ecton as under horse-keeper.

William enlisted on 27th February 1916 aged 21, he joined the Bedfordshire Regiment (Private 39845) and was called up for service on 27th February 1917 at Kettering. His occupation was given as a farm labourer. On 1st March he was posted to the 3rd Bedford Regiment and whilst there made arrangements for his mother, Mrs. A. Attwell, London Road, Earls Barton, to receive a Dependant's Allowance, which was taken regularly from his pay.

He sailed from Folkestone to France on 15th May 1917 arriving in Boulogne and marching to Calais. According to his service record he was posted to the 2nd Battalion, on 9th June 1917 and then posted to the 6th Battalion 'D' Company. He remained in France until 29th July, returning to England on the 30th when he was injured.

He went into hospital in Manchester in August 1917 and was invalided out of the army in October 1917 diagnosed with a Tubercular Spine. According to one doctor's report, originated about 1917 in England and was the result of natural causes but aggravated by active service. It was advised that sanatorium treatment was required. On 24th October 1917 he appeared before a Medical Board who awarded him 27/6d pension payable for thirty weeks to be reviewed after that. He gave his mother's address of London Road, Earls Barton, as his home address and was sent there with one pound and a new suit upon discharge. He was also awarded the Silver War Badge, given to men discharged during the war due to wounds or other incapacity.

In 1920 William Brawn married Gladys Annie F. Roe, he died in 1975 age 79.

The Brown Brothers

William Brown, a blacksmith, was born in Burniston near Scarborough, Yorkshire. In 1895 William married Ada (nee Cox) who was born in Northampton. Two of their children, Francis William and Reginald Alfred were born in Burniston. Their youngest son Arthur Leonard and two daughters, Nora Annie and Florence Irene were born in Ecton, the family having moved there in 1901.

REGINALD ALFRED BROWN (1898-1981)

Reginald was the younger brother of Francis William, who died in the war and is on the Shrine. The Roll of Honour shows Reginald had enlisted in the Northampton Regiment, however the Ecton War Book states he was in the Royal Irish Rifles. Thanks to research by Roger Storey, it was discovered that Reginald could have been part of two Drafts of soldiers who, after fourteen weeks training with the Northamptonshire Regiment were transferred to the Royal Irish Rifles 8th (Service) Battalion, East Belfast, part of the 107th Brigade, 36th Ulster Division. Unfortunately the date of the transfer is not known. According to the 1918 Absent Voters List Reginald was serving in the 11th Sussex Battalion (Private 17028). Due to the losses in the war many servicemen were transferred to different battalions when they had been depleted.

He moved away from Ecton at the end of the war and married Mabel E. Bates in the spring of 1922 and he died in Scarborough in 1981 aged 83.

JOHN CAMPION (1887-1964)

In 1891 John Campion age 3 was living in Cogenhoe with his Grandparents John and Betsey. He moved to Ecton when he was 14, where he boarded with George and Selina Jolley and their family.
At that time he was an agricultural labourer. Whilst living in Ecton he became a member of Ecton church choir. The 1911 census records he was lodging in Blacksmith's Yard, next door to the Bakery in Back Lane. He moved to the Old Bakery with his wife Mabel Jane (nee Stevenson) whom he married in the spring of 1919. There he traded as a baker and corn and flour dealer. More recently the Old Bakery was divided into two cottages, number 15 West Street and number 12 the High Street. John was a member of Ecton No. 6 Platoon Home Guard formed by Colonel Herbert Sotheby in 1945. John died aged 77 in the autumn of 1964.

According to the records, John Campion a 28 year old baker, appealed in May 1916 to the Military Tribunal (case 423N) for temporary exemption from call up on the grounds of being indispensable. The Tribunal gave him exemption until the 28th July in order to get someone else to run the bakery or close/sell it. John enlisted in the 3rd Northamptonshire Regiment at the end of July 1916 (Private 27109). The 3rd Battalion was a training battalion for drafts to the service battalions. The 3rd Battalion didn't serve abroad. The soldiers went into Labour Battalions if not acceptable for the infantry and those that went to the British Expeditionary Force (BEF) would mainly go to Northamptonshire Battalions. However they could be sent to any other needy regiment. He served at the home base until 16th November 1916 when a draft of 93 NCOs (Non-Commissioned Officers) and men from the 3rd and 16th Battalions went to France. They went to a base camp first before being sent to a battalion. At some point in his service he was transferred to the 1st Essex Regiment (Private 41455). He was discharged on 22nd November 1919. There are only two pages of his service record that have survived and they show he was in the 3rd Battalion Northamptonshire Regiment. His medal record card confirms he served with both the Northamptonshire and the Essex Regiments.

ARTHUR JOHN CLARK (1875-1938)

Arthur was the son of Joseph and Sheba Clark. Joseph a wheelwright was working in Ecton. He came originally from Little Catworth, Huntingdonshire. When he was fifteen Arthur was working as an agricultural labourer but when the 1911 census was taken he had found work as a bricklayer's labourer and was living in Back Lane, with his wife Harriet (nee Pettit) ,who he had married in 1900, their daughter Elsie Elizabeth Maud (3) and Harriet's father Job Pettit.

Arthur enlisted in the Northamptonshire Regiment (Private 17796) and went to France in 1915 with the 6th (Service) Battalion, part of the 54th Brigade, 18th Division. The 18th (Eastern) Division were formed at Colchester in September 1914 as part of the Second New Kitchener Army (K2). They arrived in France in July 1915 and served in France and Flanders until the Armistice.

On the 1918 Absent Voters List he is registered at being in the 438th Agricultural Company (Private 242041)

When he was demobilised Arthur was posted to Class Z. This meant he could return to civilian life but he knew he was obliged to return to the Army if necessary. (The Z Reserve was abolished on 31st March 1920.)

Arthur returned to live in Back Lane, Ecton and he died in the summer of 1938 aged 62 and is buried in Ecton Churchyard.

<u>GEORGE SIDNEY CLARK (1890-1959)</u>

Born in London in 1890, George worked for the Sotheby family in their house in Eaton Square, London and also in Ecton. He was confirmed in Ecton Church on 14th December 1909. In 1914 he married Nellie Ada Denton, the eldest daughter of George Denton the gamekeeper, who lived at Porter's Lodge. After the war George and Nellie moved to Sandridge near St. Albans where he had a small holding. This was not a successful venture and he accepted a

job as Verger at St. Albans Abbey and continued in this position until he died aged 60.

George served in the Royal Field Artillery and the Royal Horse Artillery, (Corporal 121696). On the 1918 Absent Voters List for Ecton, George is down as in the Divisional Ammunition Column of the Royal field Artillery (Corporal 895745).

<u>ARTHUR DARBY (1883-1949)</u>

Arthur was born in 1883, the son of Thomas, a shoemaker and his wife Ann. Thomas had died by 1901 and it is possible to see that on the remains of his service record Arthur gives his elder brother George, living at 120, Bailiff Street, Northampton, as his next of kin. There is no photograph in the Ecton War Book of Arthur but he is mentioned on the Roll of Honour in the church. In 1919 he married Violet Taylor and their son Bill attended the village school. Arthur was confirmed in Ecton Church on 10th March 1925. He was also a member of the Ecton No. 6 Platoon of the Home Guard during the Second World War. The photograph above was obtained from a group of Ecton Home Guard in 1945 outside Ecton House. (Courtesy of Rodney Ingram). Arthur was employed by the Parish Council and he carried out work at Irrigation Farm. He died aged 66 in October 1949.

Arthur enlisted in Woolwich on 6th January 1915, for a period of 3 years. Posted into the Army Service Corps as a driver (T4/038219). He was 33 years and 7 months old and his address was given as Ecton where he was working as a labourer. *There is a letter in the service records from William Smith, Steward, working for the Sotheby family, stating that Arthur worked on the Ecton Estate as a general labourer for 18 months prior to which he was working as a groom in Overstone Park and also in the stables in London. During May, June and July he was in the stables working with Mrs. Sotheby's horses as groom and gave satisfaction.*

He embarked on the SS *Southampton* on the 1st April 1915 arriving at Le Havre on the 2nd when he was posted to 28th Reserve Park. He was awarded a 1st Good Conduct Badge on 4th January 1917 and after that entry it is impossible to read the remaining service record. However the 1918 Absent Voters List shows that he was in the Army Service Corps (Dvr. 038219). A form completed in 1919 gives his permanent address at 29 Deal Street, Northampton. When he was demobilised in 1919 he was placed in Category Z and told to report to Park Royal in case of an emergency.

He returned to the village and was living in the High Street, according to the 1921 Electoral Roll.

The Darker Brothers

Maurice (born 1889) and Lewis (born 1893) were the sons of Joseph Howes Darker and Ellen (nee Croft) who were married in 1886.

LEWIS DARKER (1893-1973)

Lewis, Maurice's younger brother, was born in Ecton. At one point in his life he ran away from home to become a jockey but was brought back to work as a coachman for his father, who owned a carriage company. (This Information was taken from Ecton a Northamptonshire Parish. Courtesy of Rodney Ingram.) In 1911, age 17, he was working as a groom, for Thomas Collier a farmer in Hanging Houghton, Northampton. In 1920 he married Dorothy Ethel Reeve they lived in West Haddon and had six children. Lewis died age 80 in 1973, Dorothy died in 1982.

Lewis enlisted into the Northamptonshire Yeomanry, (Private 944) later re-numbered (Private 145246). He served with the Yeomanry for the duration of the war.

The 1/1 Battalion Northamptonshire Yeomanry Regiment was formed on the 4th August 1914, with the Headquarters, Machine Gun Section and four Squadrons under the command of Lieutenant Colonel H. Wickham. The Machine Gun Section had two 303 inch converted Maxim guns. 'A' Squadron plus one machine gun were based in Northampton. 'B' Squadron at Peterborough, 'C' at Kettering and 'D' plus the other machine gun at Daventry. 'D' was eventually utilised to complete the other Squadrons, also to provide mounted police for the North Midland Division.

On 10th August the 1/1 was entrained to the war station at Derby, then on the 15th to the North Midland Division at Luton. Lewis was billeted at Houghton Regis. In September they were sent to the 7th Division in the New Forest for overseas service and were the first Yeomanry Battalion selected to go. To their disappointment this order was cancelled in favour of the Northumberland Hussars, as the whole of the personnel of the Hussars, had signed the Imperial Service Obligation prior to the 4th August. This was signed when territorial troops agreed to serve abroad, something they were not obliged to do before the war. So the Hussars took precedence over the 7th Division.

On the 1st October 1914 the 1/1 were sent to join the 8th Division and the 2/1 Battalion was raised to take their place at the home establishment, under Colonel C.H.E. Coote. They trained at Towcester and provided reinforcements for the 1/1 in the field. Later the 3/1 was raised.

On the 4th November the 1/1 received orders to stop all training and prepare to move. They were marched to Southampton and embarked for France arriving at Le Havre, camping on the cliffs on 6th November 1914, Lewis Darker, as his medal card shows, was part of this contingent. They moved to the fighting line in Merille, Estairs Sector and were there for the whole of the winter.

The Yeomanry spent the winter of 1914/15 digging trenches and making good damage, occasionally relieving the infantry in the trenches. They were billeted at Lestrem. In February 1915 the Battalion relieved the 2nd Battalion Northamptonshire Regiment in 'C' lines sector of Neuve Chappell to enable the Northamtonshires to rest and prepare for an offensive. The Yeomanry were relieved from this duty on Saturday 6th March at 9pm. On the 7th March they were placed under the orders of 24th Infantry Brigade and they took over the 'D' lines sector of the trench system.

The 8th Division Cyclist Company and the Yeomanry, as dismounted mounted troops, under the command of Lieutenant Colonel M. Windam held the line between 7th and 8th Divisions (IV Corps) in the battle of Neuve Chappell. The Machine Gun Section was attached to the Cyclist Section.

On 11th April 1917 the Yeomanry were ordered to proceed to Orange Hill to cover the left flank of 45th Infantry Brigade during an attack on Monchy Le Preux. They were heavily shelled before they advanced, in open order, under further intensive shellfire in the one and a half mile dash for Monchy. However, they gained their objective and enabled the infantry to get over in sufficient numbers to hold it. They spent the night in the German dugouts beneath the Arras triangle.

Later they went to Italy and joined the XIV Corps Cavalry Regiment. In April 1918 the XIV Corps became the G.H.Q. British Force in Italy and the unit became the G.H.Q. troops. In October 1918 XlV Corps was reformed and again became Corps Cavalry Regiment until the end of the war.

<u>MAURICE DARKER (1889-1969)</u>

Maurice *was born in Ecton. According to his family he went to Rawalpindi in India before the First World War. Unfortunately there are no surviving records. After the war he married Charlotte Manning in Brixworth and she died there in 1964. Maurice died on 13th December 1969 also in Brixworth, aged 80.*

Maurice's medal card states he served in the Royal Wiltshire Yeomanry, Staffordshire Yeomanry and 1st Company of London Yeomanry (Private 2009). He was also in the Company of Hussars (Private261587) during 1915. There are no surviving service records, the 1918 Absent Voters List records him in City Londons (Private 321383). He left the village after the war.

The Dexters

Thomas and his brother Samuel, who died and is commemorated on the Shrine, were two of the ten children of George Dexter, a stockman and Rebecca (nee Thorpe), who married in 1870 and were living in the High Street, Ecton, in 1911.

THOMAS HENRY DEXTER (1899-1957)

Like his brother Samuel and father, George, Thomas worked as a stockman. He was employed by Mr Dicks of South Lodge. In 1913 Thomas married Ada Tingle. He returned to the village after the war and lived in Back Lane. He died in 1957 age 69, Ada died on 10th November 1966 and they are buried in Ecton Churchyard.

According to the Ecton War Book he joined the 3rd Battalion Royal Sussex Regiment (Private 34128). This Reserve Battalion was formed in Chichester on 4th August 1914 and went to Dover. In May 1915 it went to Newhaven and remained in Newhaven Garrison. His name is added near the bottom of the Roll of Honour in the church and not in alphabetical order, as are the other men, so he possibly did not enlist until near the end of the war. On the Roll of Honour he is given as joining the Army Service Corps.

JOHN DRUMMOND (1874-1931)

John was born in 1874 in Muthill, Perthshire, his father John was a mason. In 1891 John was working as a groom and in 1901, aged 25, he was employed by William Henderson of Balbirnie Stables in Markinch. This was near to property in Scotland owned by the Sotheby family. By 1907 John was employed as a groom/coachman for the Sotheby's and had moved to Ecton. In 1907 he married Florence Hanwick Labrum. Florence had been born in Ecton and brought her two sons, Harold Alfred and Ernest Walter Labrum, to the marriage. Between 1908 and 1915 John and Florence had five children, two daughters and three sons. According to Suie Rands, John Drummond acted as barber to the village boys. After the war he continued to live in Ecton where he died on 28th July 1931 aged 57. He and Florence are buried in Ecton Churchyard.

John went to France on 14th February 1915 with the Army Service Corps (Private M2/047406) this was later renumbered and on the Absent Voters List of 1918 he was registered as in the Heavy Transport Division of the Army Service Corps (Dvr. 421993). He was discharged on 28th May 1919, Class "Z". *Returning to live in High Street, Ecton where his children went to school and were confirmed in the local church.*

The Army Service Corps supplied the materials of war to the fighting soldier. They were essential to the running of the war. The first companies were formed to work in the supply depots at French ports and two days after the first company was formed on 24th August 1914 they arrived in France. They also served in Salonika and the UK. In June 1917 they were transferred to the Labour Corps.

CECIL ALBERT V. EALES (1894-1939)

Cecil was born in Hardingstone. His father Stephen, worked as a carter at the local brewery and according to the 1911 census the family were living at 113 Everton Road, Northampton, Cecil, aged 17 was working as a general labourer.

Cecil enlisted in the Northamptonshire Yeomanry, 'A' Division (Private 145227) stationed in Northampton. In 1918 he had been promoted to Corporal, according to the Absent Voters List. He was later promoted to Sergeant and his service number changed (918). He and Lewis Darker had the same experiences in France. Cecil was mentioned in the Regimental War Diary. During the attack on Monchy Sergeant C.A.V. Eales was recorded as wounded.

Whilst on leave in the summer of 1917 Cecil married Mabel Harris, his father's occupation was given as Licensed Victualler. After the war Cecil and Mabel lived in the village until Cecil's death on 19th January 1939 aged 44. His burial service was conducted in Ecton Church and in the churchyard Cecil, his wife, elder brother and parents are remembered on a memorial stone.

ISAAC FISHER (1883-1959)

Like John Drummond, Isaac Fisher is recorded both on the Roll of Honour and in the Ecton War Book as enlisting in the Army Service Corps. There is no record of his living in Ecton before 1911. On the 1911 census he is recorded as born in Hitcham, Suffolk and married for two years to Florence (nee Butler, also born in Suffolk). They were living in Back Lane, Ecton and Isaac was working as a stockman. He later returned to Suffolk and died in Gipping in the autumn of 1959 age 76.

Isaac's service records unfortunately have not survived and he is not recorded on any of the voter's lists after 1915 and had presumably moved away.

SAMUEL LAW FITZHUGH (1884-1965)

Samuel Fitzhugh was born in Ecton and lived in Front Street with his parents George Fitzhugh and Elizabeth (nee Law). In a cottage now lived in by Jayne Wiggins, the hairdresser. At the age of 17 he was working with his father as a shoemaker, although on the 1911 census he gives his occupation as stone mason. In 1910 he married Nellie Tebby, the daughter of Thomas and Elizabeth Tebby. They had four daughters Doris and Phyllis born before the war, Kathleen (1916) and Elsie (1921). They lived in 55 Melville Street, Northampton. Samuel served in the Ecton Home Guard during the Second World War. He died on 29th May 1965 aged 81 and Nellie in 1985 aged 100; they are buried in Ecton Churchyard.

Samuel enlisted in the Royal Field Artillery (Driver 234472). Sadly his service records have not survived. The 1918 and 1919 Absent Voters Lists register him as being in the Divisional Artillery Column S.A.A.B

The Royal Field Artillery supported the cavalry and infantry, so Samuel would have been in the thick of the fighting, trying to scythe down the enemy who were attacking in the open. The lighter guns used by the artillery fired high explosive shells and their equipment was a complete gun carriage and limber mounted on wheels.

The Royal Regiment of Artillery, (Royal Horse Artillery, Royal Field Artillery and Royal Garrison Artillery), was split into two groups in 1899.The Royal Horse Artillery and Royal Field Artillery forming one group and the Royal Garrison Artillery, used for coastal defence and heavy guns into the other. They were not re-amalgamated until 1924.

After being discharged from the army Samuel continued to live in the village.

JOHN MICHAEL FORTUNE (1886-1971)

John Michael Fortune was born in December 1886 in Teignmouth, Devon. He was the son of Patrick Fortune born in County Meath, Ireland and Charlotte who was born in Chelsea, Middlesex. Patrick Fortune worked as a butler and the family moved from Devon to Hertfordshire then to London. There is a record of John Michael being confirmed in 1909 in Wellingborough Parish Church by the Bishop of Peterborough along with other men from Ecton. He was recorded on the 1911 census as working as a domestic servant for Mrs. Sotheby. In 1913 he married Eleanor E. Gibbins in Northampton. After 1919 he is not listed on the Electoral Rolls for Ecton and died in the Peterborough area in the spring of 1971 aged 87.

He enlisted in the Royal Garrison Artillery (Gunner 194697) in 1919. He was in the 102nd Seige Battery Royal Garrison Artillery. Later he was promoted to Sergeant.

CHARLES FREEMAN 1885 - 1946

Charles Freeman born in Stanwick, Northamptonshire, was the son of William Freeman and Mary (nee Jellis). In 1901 age 15 Charles was working as a journeyman baker. He married Esther Irena Tebby in 1907 and was registered in the 1911 census working as a full time baker, living in the Co-operative Store in Ecton. The Co-operative Store was originally the School for Poor Children erected in 1752 by John Palmer. The Co-operative Society leased the building in 1878 after the school had closed and they traded there for about a hundred years. Charles and Esther lived there with their two children, Gladys Irena (1909) and William Thomas (1912). After the war he returned to Ecton.

Charles was called up into the Army Service Corps in September 1916 and applied (like John Campion) for an exemption on the grounds it was in the National Interest that he remain working as a baker in the village and not go into the Army. (Case N1037). He was given a temporary exemption until 22nd November when he joined the bakery section of the 237th Army Service Corps (Private S/219000).

Charles Freeman spent all his service life in England.

His service record shows he was thirty years and four months when he enlisted. There is a certificate dated 4th November 1916 which states "Charles Freeman had been tested in "K" (Supply) Company

Field Bakery in Aldershot and proved himself." (*He obviously rose to the occasion*). His service sheet shows he joined the S4 Bakery Section ASC Manchester 4th July 1917. It is very faded and difficult to see where he was before that. He was issued with the following items:

Clothing - Boots, (ankle, pairs 2); Caps (Service Dress 1); Drawers (pairs 2); Greatcoat (D.M. 1); Jackets (Service Dress 2); Putties (pairs 1); Trousers (Service Dress pairs 2); Waistcoat (cardigan 1). Necessaries – Badge (cap 1); Bag (Kit 1); Braces (pairs 1); Brass Button (1); Brush, (Brass 1); Brush (Blacking 1); Brush (Clothes 1); Brush (Hair 1); Brush (Polishing 1); Brush (Shaving 1); Brush (Tooth 1); Cap (Comforter 1); Comb (hair 1); Disc.(identity, with cord 1); Fork (1); Holdall (1); Housewife (1, this is a small sewing kit); Knife (Table 1); Laces (leather spare, pairs 1); Shirts (flannel 3); Socks (worsted, pairs 3); Spoon (1); Titles (metal pairs 1); Towels (hand 1); Wax Polish (tin 1).

He was transferred to the reserve and discharged from the Army on 13th October 1919. He continued to live in the village.

ANDREW YOUNG GRAY (1887-1934)

Andrew was the youngest son of William Gray and Margaret (nee Young), he was born in Kelson, Roxburgh and lived there until joining the Seaforth Highlanders. His father became gamekeeper to the Sotheby family, who had an estate in Scotland through their

connection with the McMillan-Scot family. William, his wife and younger daughter lived in Keepers cottage in Ecton and were later joined by Andrew who came to work with his father. Andrew married Edith Minna Summerfield, the daughter of William Summerfield. Andrew was buried on 28th October 1934 aged 47, his wife Edith on 27th July 1940 aged 57 they are buried in Ecton churchyard. There are no surviving service records. The Absent Voters List for Ecton in 1918 registers Andrew as living in Keepers House and serving in the Royal Engineers (Corporal 246348).

ALBERT VICTOR GREY (1898-1932)

Albert Victor was the eldest son of Nat and Ethel Minerva (nee Barritt). His family had lived in Ecton for many years and in 1911 his father was a milkman on a local farm.

According to the Ecton War Book Albert enlisted in August 1916 into the Machine Gun Corps and the 1918 Absent Voters List says 36th Machine Gun Corps (Private 133226). He was discharged in February 1919. He was twice wounded during the time he served. The Roll of Honour states he enlisted into the Northamptonshire Regiment. So far it has been difficult to verify either of these statements as there are no remaining service records. The 1916 Northamptonshire Independent has a photograph showing that he was in the 7th Machine Gun Corps.

After the war Albert returned to the village where he was recorded on the Electoral Rolls until 1921. He went to live in the Cambridge area but later moved to Surrey where he died in 1932.

<u>JOHN HENRY HALL (1899-1937)</u>

Known as Harry, John Henry lived in High Street, Ecton with his parents James Thomas and Nanny Stevens Hall and his surviving sister Marjorie (1903), her twin sister Lily died at birth. James Thomas worked as a groom in the Livery Stables. John Henry Hall died 9th June 1937.

According to the Roll of Honour, Harry enlisted at the end of the war into the Army of Occupation. Although his photograph appears in the Ecton War Book there are no details included about his regiment or involvement in the church. He is registered on the 1919 Absent Voters List as being in 51st Bedfordshire Regiment (Private 52594). When the Armistice was declared John Hall may have been amongst the men who went on into Germany.

FREDERICK WALTER HARLOTT (1891-1969)

Frederick's grandfather, Daniel Harlott, was born in Great Billing and moved to Ecton where he worked for Arthur Childs, living with the Childs family at The Lodge, Main Street. In 1859 he married Lucy Randall, they had two children, Herbert John (1866) and Elizabeth (1869) plus Lucy's son, Joseph Randall, (1851).

Frederick's father, Herbert John, married Elizabeth Tebbutt in 1887, they had six children, one of whom died young. In 1901 they were living in Box Cottage, High Street, Ecton with their daughters Winifred (13), Elsie (7), Constance (2 days old when the census was taken) and their son Frederick Walter (10).

Frederick was a church bell ringer and he is on the photograph in the Belfry titled "Patriotic Bell Ringers". In 1921 Frederick married Evelyn M. Robinson, they had four children, Gwendolene M. (1922), Herbert F. (1923), Geoffrey W. (Geoff), (1928) and Leonard J. (1929).

After the war Frederick returned to the village. Working for Mr. Dicks and acting as the Verger for 50 years. He was also a member of the Ecton Home Guard No. 6 Platoon, in the Second World War. He died in 1969 at the age of 79 and is buried in Ecton Churchyard.

Frederick enlisted in the Northamptonshire Yeomanry, 'C' Squadron (1521) on 24th November 1914. He was in the second draft sent from Towcester to Lesbrern on 21st February 1915. In April of that year the Squadron were at Boescheppe, eight miles west of Ypres. Here on 22nd April they acted as traffic controllers in Poperinghe later moving to Vlamertinghe. They returned to Boescheppe and provided working parties in the vicinity of Zillebeke and Hill 60. Frederick was wounded on 20th July 1915 and sent to 13 Field Ambulance for treatment. He later moved with the Squadron to Hondeschem and then Mericourt. They were billeted at Busay Les Douars and provided patrols reconnoitring the front line position. In August the Squadron set up posts on the River Somme to prevent British and French troops crossing into each other's territory.

During their time in France they joined Officer's patrols and made reconnaissance patrols along the Somme also manning night observation posts.

On the 1st January 1916 they took over the Dragon Wood defences with patrols keeping in touch with the French Territorial Brigade holding Frize. By 1918 according to the Ecton Absent Voters List he was still with the 1st Northamptonshire Yeomanry but had been re-numbered (Tpr. 145673).

When he was demobbed Frederick received a certificate from The Territorial Force Association of the County of Northampton in thanks for his services in the Great War of 1914-1919.

GEORGE HARSENT (1880-1963)

George was the son of Henry Harsent and Sarah J. He was born in Badingham, Suffolk. George married Edith Annie the daughter of Charles Hensman and Mary Ann (nee Taylor) who had been born in Ecton. The Hensman family had moved from Ecton to Kings Bromley and in 1901 Charles was a Farm Bailiff, at Fisherwick Farm, Fisherwick, Staffordshire. George and Edith were married in Staffordshire in 1902, living there with their first child, Elsie, (1904). By the time they had their second daughter, Edith, (1907) the family were living in High Street, Ecton. The cottage is now the home of the Kilpin family. George died in 1963.

George served with the Royal Fusiliers and on 4th December a list of Honours and Awards was received by the Regiment and (Private 96348) G. Harsent was awarded the Military Medal. A letter was received by the Regiment's Commanding Officer at the Battalion HQ, Dompierre, France, from Major General Sir G. Barton, K.C.V.O. C.B. C.M.G. Colonel of the Regiment:- *"I wish to congratulate all ranks of the Third Battalion on their splendid record of Service, both on the Western Front and in Salonica, as well as on their many brilliant engagements which have added glory to the History of the Regiment"* (Royal Fusiliers War Diary, December 4th 1918). The award was recorded in the Supplement to the London Gazette 23rd July 1919.

According to his medal card and the Absent Voters List in 1918 George also served with the 9th Royal Lancashire Regiment (Private 26346).

The Hensman Family

The Hensmans were one of the oldest Ecton families, they are recorded in Ecton in the 16th Century.

Thomas Hensman (born in Ecton 1792) must have served in the Militia as he was a Chelsea Pensioner, he married Dorothy (born Ireland 1799) they had two sons:

Charles, the youngest (1831), married Sarah Randall in 1850, their son Thomas died in 1911.

George the eldest, (1828) married Harriet Elson in 1849. The eldest of their nine children, John Elson Hensman (1851) married first Sophia Creamer in 1870, they had two children, Frederick, who served the Militia in South Africa but was not in the village in the First World War, also a daughter Annie. After Sophie's death John Elson married her sister Martha in 1883 and their son Edgar Herbert died in the war and is commemorated with the men on the Shrine.

George's youngest son Alfred (born 1863) married Angelina Jenkins in 1886. (known as Lina or Eleanor). Alfred had numerous jobs. In 1880 he was living in Kings Bromley and working as a gardener. Ten years later he was back in Northampton and working as an attendant to the Insane in St. Andrews Hospital, Northampton. In 1901 Alfred and Angelina were living at the Plough Hotel, Bridge Street, Northampton where Alfred was working as the caretaker. They moved to the Three Horseshoes Public House in Ecton with their sons. Horace (1896), one of the bell ringers mentioned on the plaque in the Belfry, he died in the war and is commemorated on the Shrine. Percy their second son was born 1900 and later they had a third son, George Edward Lionel and a daughter Dorothy Grace. The family moved to Leicester to take over the Old Crown Inn in Shearsby and then to the Chandlers Arms, also in Shearsby. Lionel was too young to fight although he tried to enlist but was turned down.

PERCY HAROLD GEORGE HENSMAN (1900-1971)

According to the information given in the Ecton War Book, Percy was "a well-made lad, who joined up when he was 15 years and 8 months old" it also states" he had 4 months of 'trench foot' before he was 17". His service record, one of the few that has survived, is incomplete and barely legible. It states on the first page that Percy joined up at 19. However the Medical History page shows clearly that the age had been altered. So it is possible when he went to enlist he was told he was too young then told by the recruiting sergeant "if he went round the block he might find he had aged"! This he must have done as he was accepted into the army. His family must have agreed to his enlisting, otherwise as an underage soldier his Mother could have applied to the Authorities and had him sent back home. He was 5' 5"tall and well developed and was living at the time of his enlistment at Old Crown Inn, Shearsby, Leicestershire. Later his address changed to Chandlers Arms, Shearsby, near Rugby. He had been working in Leicester as a Hosiery Hand. His mother was given as his next of kin.

He enlisted in the 11th Battalion Leicester Pioneers (Private 21597) on 16th October 1915 and served in France with the British Expeditionary Force in 1916. He was admitted to hospital on 19th December 1916 and spent 82 days there with trench foot. He was admitted again on 20th March 1917 staying until 11th June 1917 with the same complaint.

In 1918 he was transferred to the 5th Battalion Rifle Brigade (B/2000030) as Acting Bugler (paid) and in August of that year posted to the 2nd Battalion at Rugley, Staffordshire. He retained the rank of Lance Corporal (paid) and was discharged from service 31st March 1920 receiving a pension of £12-1s-11d for the period of one year.

In 1929 Percy married Alice M. Lines at Billesdon in Leicestershire and he died in Leicester in 1971.

ARTHUR JAMES (1885-1960)

Arthur was born in Wollaston, one of the ten children of John James and Charlotte (nee Johnson, born in Ecton). Charlotte was the daughter of Fanny and George Johnson. In 1861 Fanny was the village Post lady.
There is no mention of Arthur anywhere on the 1911 census. His Father states in the 1911 census that he had ten children all of whom were still living. According to the Ecton War Book Arthur was a lay worker and a reader and he joined the Royal Army Medical Corps. Unfortunately there are too many Arthur James to distinguish which one he is.
In 1919 he married Beatrice Knight, and he died aged 79 in 1960.

The Johnson Family

George Johnson (born 1824, Ecton), a Tailor, married Francis Kingston in 1853. Their elder son Charles (1853) married Rachel Smith in 1874, they had eight children and their sons, Frederick Charles, Wentworth, Harry Lionel (who died in the war and is commemorated on the Shrine) and Bertram Sydney all fought in the First World War.

BERTRAM SIDNEY JOHNSON (1892-1972)

Bertram was one of the Ecton Patriotic Bell Ringers whose photograph hangs in the Belfry.

Bertram, the youngest of the Johnson brothers to fight in the war, enlisted at Northampton in 1914 into the Northamptonshire Yeomanry. Together with a number of men from Ecton he was initially in "C" Squadron. According to the Regimental Diary he joined at the same time as Cecil Eales, Frederick Harlott, James Lewer, Thomas Mallard, Albert Roddis and Arthur Luck. (Lewis Darker and Ernest Stubbs also served with the Yeomanry). It was almost an 'Ecton Pals' Squadron. In May 1916 some of the same group were transferred to the Northamptonshire Regiment.

The Regimental Diary records that Bertram Johnson was wounded but unfortunately does not give details. The Ecton War Book also states that Bertram was wounded and that he served for a time in

Italy. The Squadron went to Italy on 10th November 1917 and became part of the General Headquarters Troops.

The 1918 Absent Voters List registers Bertram in 1st Northamptonshire Regiment (Private 145682).

Returning home after the war Bertram worked as a painter and plumber. In 1928 he married Mercy Robinson. Their son Lionel Charles married his cousin Sylvia Violet Johnson, who is still living in the village today. Bertram served as a Corporal in the Ecton No. 6 Platoon of the Home Guard during the Second World War. Bertram died on 28th December 1972 aged 80.

WENTWORTH JOHNSON (1878)

On 29th October 1900 aged 21 years and 11 months Wentworth enlisted at Northampton. When asked if he had at any time belonged to Her Majesty's Army he replied that he had been with the 3rd Battalion of the Northamptonshire Regiment and the Militia, with which he was still serving. He applied to join the Royal Regiment of Artillery. He was posted to India in September 1901 (Private 12088) and discharged in October 1912. Upon his discharge Wentworth emigrated to Canada and in September 1914 enlisted in the 1st Battalion Canadian Overseas Expeditionary Force (No. 6984). He was wounded and discharged in April 1915 his medical case sheet states:

Bullet wound in the back, scapular region. On 23rd April while advancing to make a counter attack near Flers he received a bullet wound in the back, lay on the field about five hours when under the cover of darkness he made his way about half a mile to the dressing station. Had the wound dressed then walked about two miles to a village (name unknown), got into a motor ambulance and rode about six miles to a large dressing station (name unknown). Had the wound dressed and remained overnight, leaving next morning by motor to a town (name unknown), had the wound dressed in hospital then proceeded by train to Boulogne arriving Sunday morning. Wound well attended to. He left Wednesday morning for Cliveden via Southampton.

Inspection: Colour and nutrition good, teeth, most of upper jaw gone .
Personal History: Had syphilis twelve years ago but had it cleared up under T.T.
Physical examination: heart and lungs in good condition
Present condition: May 10th 1915 Patient has a bullet wound entering just over inner and upper corner of right scapula and producing point of exit left scapula, wound is about three inches long, two inches wide. Moist dressings were applied. The report goes on to state the various stages of the healing and finishes on June 24 when both wounds are healed and he was recommended for convalescence at home. He was discharged to Bromley.
Whether 'Home' meant he was sent back to Canada or whether he was sent to his parents in Ecton is not stated.

By November 20th 1917, Wentworth was back in Canada at 407 Confederation Street, Sarnia, Ontario, and he re-enlisted in Lenion, Ontario, where he was considered fit for overseas service. Unfortunately there are no more records to show his further service.
According to the shipping records, Wentworth visited England in September 1927. Sailing from Quebec and arriving in London.

FRANK BLAXLEY JOHNSON (1890)

George and Frances Johnson's younger son Frank was the village Postmaster (taking over the post from his Mother). He married

89

Sarah Blaxley in 1887. Their sons Frank, Percy and Sydney all fought in the First World War. The remaining brothers Cyril and Frederick were too young.

Frank the eldest of the brothers worked for the Sotheby family as a gardener and in the 1911 census was registered as living at The Stables, Ecton House. Frank was very involved in the life of the church, as a member of the choir, an altar server and one of the Patriotic Bell Ringers.

Frank enlisted into the Northamptonshire Yeomanry (Private 145683) and was transferred to the Bedfordshire Yeomanry (Private 31213). Unfortunately there are no surviving service records. The Bedfordshire Yeomanry served in France and Flanders. The 1918 Absent Voters List registers Frank in 12th Lancers (Private 145683).

Unfortunately as there are so many Frank Johnsons born around the same time it has not been possible to find details of a marriage or the date of death.

PERCY ARTHUR JOHNSON (1891)

Percy worked as a groom and lived at home. He was a member of the church choir.

Percy enlisted in Northampton into the Royal Engineers, Railway Company. These companies were engaged all over the British

Sector and their main objective was to take a standard gauge railway as close to the front as possible to enable troops and ammunition to be moved forward and casualties back away from the line.

The Light Railway Division had prefabricated lengths of line which could be laid with the minimum amount of ground work, easily carried and assembled quickly.

There are no service records for Percy Arthur Johnson and two medal cards, both for Percy A. Johnson in the Royal Engineers and it is impossible to sort out which is the Ecton one also he is not on either the 1918 or 1919 Register of Absent Voters.

Percy Arthur married Winifred M. Briggs in Northampton in 1920 and moved away from the village.

SIDNEY JOHNSON (1896)

Sidney, younger brother of Frank and Percy, was baptised in Ecton in August 1896 and confirmed in April 1910. He was a member of the church choir, a bell ringer and altar server.

He enlisted into the Norfolk Regiment (Private 13061) serving in France in October 1915. He was wounded in 1916, 1917 and 1918 and discharged from active service on 27th March 1918.

Sydney had received wounds affecting the nerves in his left hand, which was clenched tightly for ten months. After a fortnight of constant massage at home in Ecton his fingers released and he regained the use of his hand.

According to the Ecton War Book Sidney was transferred at some point from the Norfolk Regiment to the Leicestershire Regiment

After the war Sidney moved away from the village and lived in Earls Barton.

HORACE GEORGE JOHNSON (1896)

Horace George was the son of George Johnson and Harriet Esther (nee Labrum) and was born in 1896 in Ecton. In 1911 he was living with his parents in Ecton and working as a house painter. He was a member of the church choir and he also rang the bells although he is not on the photograph of the Patriotic Bell Ringers. On 20th October 1909 he was confirmed by the Bishop of Leicester and in 1925 he married Jane Artherton.

Horace enlisted in the 2nd Northamptonshire Regiment (Private 27771, in 1919 he was renumbered 70488). After the war he went to live in Barnet then went to Rossendale, Lancs.

<u>The Jolley Family</u>

Amos' father George Jolley was born in 1831. He and his first wife, Mary Ann (nee Butts), had eight sons, one of these, Ernest James died in the war and is commemorated on the Shrine. After Mary Ann's death George re-married in 1875 to Selina (nee Burditt). They had three daughters, Annie (1877), Clara (1878), Rose (1881) and a son, Amos (1883)

<u>AMOS JOLLEY (1883-1955)</u>

Amos worked as a teamster on a local farm and in 1903 he married Ada Florence Darby. Ada had been working at The World's End, Ecton, for William Perkins, Licensee. Her family lived in Cogenhoe where in 1904 Amos and Ada's son Russell was born. By the time of the 1911 census the family were living in Back Lane, Ecton. Ada Jolley died in 1937 and Amos in 1955.

According to the Roll of Honour in Ecton Church, Amos Jolley joined the Royal Fusiliers and according to the Ecton War Book, he joined the Labour Battalion, Army Service Corps. As there are no surviving service records for him or a medal card it is difficult to trace his military service. In his photograph in the Ecton War Book his cap badge is of the Royal Fusiliers. He is registered in the 1918 and 1919 Absent Voters Lists as 106th Royal Fusiliers (Private 6383).

PERCY CHARLES JOLLEY (1895-1972)

Percy Charles was born in Ecton in 1895 the eldest son of Henry and Mabel (nee Austin). He worked as a dairyman. In 1913 he married Florence K. Riseley.

When he was 19, giving his occupation as farm labourer and his mother as next of kin, Percy joined the Territorial Force, for one year's embodied service at home (Private T1217). Although the Territorial Force was originally for men serving only in the United Kingdom, on 9th September 1914, Percy signed an agreement (Army Form E.624) to serve in any place outside the United Kingdom in the event of National Emergency. He went into the East Midlands Brigade, East Anglian Division as a driver in the Army Service Corps. His limited service was reckoned from the date of his attestation, 4th August 1914, this service was completed after one year and a hundred and nine days when he was discharged in November 1915.

He re-enlisted immediately at Boxmoor on 20th November 1915, (Private 21846).This service was for the duration of the War, his occupation is given as dairyman and on the attestation form his father Henry, was given as his next of kin.

He served at home until 29th January 1916 when he went with the Northampton 1/4 Battalion to Salonika on 30th January 1916 where they stayed until 20th September 1917.

Two of the forms with the documents of his service record that survive, show a remarkable distain for authority. He was confined to barracks on a number of occasions and in total had 21 days field punishment No.1 and his pay docked. For offences ranging from neglect of duty whilst on guard in Boxmoor to being improperly dressed on parade, not cleaning his lance and losing the point of the lance and being insolent to an officer whilst serving abroad on active service. There were two sheets of offences in England and abroad from 1915 until 1918. Also surviving is: (Army Form W.3226) Particulars to Character of Soldier serving with an Expeditionary Force who is sent home for discharge or permanently for any reason (the form will be signed by the Soldier's Commanding Officer) on this form under no.6 –Any other facts regarding him you wish to be noted? It states: "While with this Unit his character has been excellent. Was a very clean soldier and very keen."

On November 27th 1918 the family in Ecton received a War Office Telegram telling them that Percy had died in hospital in Alexandria. They must have been devastated. However, the next document in the records is a letter from Mrs. Jolley to the War Office:

"Sir, On November 27, I received from Warley (Army Form W.3038) information of the death of my son (Private 48216) Percy Charles Jolley. Thank GOD it was a mistake for I have a letter from him dated December 2nd from the hospital in Alexandria.
I give you this information and request that you will rectify the money transactions which may have begun on the supposed death of my son. M.A.Jolley"
This is followed by a copy of a second letter to the War Office:

"Sir I beg to inform you that my son Percy Charles Jolley (Private 48216) 1/4 Northants. Regiment. Is alive not-withstanding the notice of his death sent to me by you. (Army Form B. 104-82). I had a letter from him dated the 2nd December last from the hospital in

Alexandria. Moreover Mr.M.Haynes of Earls Barton saw him in the hospital alive and getting better of malaria on November 16th whereas the telegram says Died in November 13th.
Yours faithfully M.A.Jolley

The War Office inter-office memo states that on the report, from which the original telegram was sent, "died" is an error which is regretted.

A further memo says the error occurred because the wording on the form was read as died instead of diseased and is regretted. On the Absent Voters List in 1918 Percy was registered in the Heavy Transport Division of the Army Service Corps (Dvr. 160558). Percy was discharged early from service on 9th April 1919.

REGINALD JOLLEY (1898)

There are no existing service records for Reginald Jolley, the younger brother of Percy. The Roll of Honour says he served with Royal Irish Rifles (8/41536). It is possible that Percy was part of one or two drafts of the Northamptonshire Regiment which were transferred to the Royal Irish Rifles after an initial fourteen weeks training. His battalion became part of the 107th Brigade, 36th Ulster Division fighting in France. Whilst with this division he would have been in a number of hard fought battles especially at Beaumont Hamel. The 8th and 9th Battalions of the Royal Irish Rifles were amalgamated in August 1917 to become the 8/9 battalion and were eventually disbanded in February 1918, the men being transferred to other Royal Irish Rifle Battalions. The 1918 and 1919 Absent Voters List registered Reginald in 3rd Royal Irish Division (Rfn 41536). He returned home after demobilisation.

The Knatt Family

James and Charles were the sons of Wilfrid Knatt and Mary Ann (nee Randall). They had two step-brothers, Frederick H. Randall and Thomas G. Randall. Although the family were Baptists, both James and his younger brother Charles are mentioned in the Ecton War Book. In 1911 the family were living in Blacksmiths Yard, Ecton with their lodger John Campion, the baker mentioned previously.

CHARLES WILFRED KNATT (1892-1946)

Charles enlisted in the East Kent Regiment (The Buffs) (G/21100). There are no service records for him but according to the Ecton War Book he was taken prisoner and spent time in a camp in Germany. There are no records available of his time as a prisoner. On the 1918 and 1919 Absent Voters List Charles registered address was given as Blacksmiths Yard.

In 1920 Charles visited his brother James and step-brother Frederick in Canada, later returning to England and marrying Dorothy C. Anderson in 1932 and living in Brixworth until his death in 1946.

JAMES ANTHONY KNATT (1890)

James, the elder brother of Charles went to Canada in April 1910 to visit his step-brother Frederick Randall, who had emigrated in March 1908. James emigrated in May 1910 and both he and Frederick were allowed a British Bonus to cover their emigration. They went to Canada to farm.

James enlisted in the Canadian Overseas Expeditionary Force on 21st February 1916, he gave his step-brother Fred Randall as his next of kin and at that time James lived at Strathmore, Alberta and Fred at 2625 Thirteenth St. N.W. Highbury, Calgary.

He returned to live in Canada after the war.

HAROLD ALFRED LABRUM (1899-1979)

Harold was the son of Florence Hanwick Labrum and step-son of John Drummond. Harold was a bell ringer according to the Ecton War Book, although he is not listed on the lists of ringers which hang in the Belfry. He was confirmed in November 1913. In 1923 he married Ethel Kate Eales and he died in 1979.

Harold enlisted into the Royal Navy Volunteer Reserve as a signaller. There are no records existing for his service. However the 1918 Absent Voters List registered Harold as serving at Devonport Royal Military Barracks (6782).

HARRY WOODLEY LESTER (1909-1971)

Harry was the son of Thomas William Lester, a retired Civil Servant (born Marylebone 1859) and Kate (nee Edgecombe, born Totnes

99

1864). The family came to Ecton around 1909 and Harry became a member of the Ecton Football Club and joined the choir. He worked for Mr. Green the undertaker and when Mr.Green died and his son moved to Earls Barton and couldn't afford to continue to employ Harry, so Harry set up on his own as Wheelwright and Undertaker in the village. He also helped as an assistant to Andrew Gray the gamekeeper. He married Violet May Tomkins, a parlour maid in Ecton Hall. Mrs. Sotheby was a witness at the wedding in February 1918. In 1946/7 Harry was the Chairman of the Parish Council. His wife and parents are buried in the Ecton Churchyard and although Harry is remembered on the headstone, he insisted that he didn't want to be buried in the churchyard but wanted his ashes scattered in the garden of the home in West Street where he had lived.

Harry Lester enlisted in the Army Service Corps (Private A/367929). According to his daughter Jean Leigh he did not serve abroad. The Absent Voters List of 1918 registered him in the Army Service Corps Motor Transport (Private 323753).

JAMES AMOS LEWER (1896-1971)

James, known as Amos, Lewer was born in Dorking, Surrey; his parents were Thomas Job Lewer and Emma (nee Carter). In 1917 he married Hester S. Bartlett and whilst in Ecton he worked as a butler to the Sotheby family. He died in 1971 in Horsham, Sussex.

Amos enlisted into the Northamptonshire Yeomanry on the 24th November 1914, Troop 1 C Squadron (Private 1537, later 145058) giving his father in Dorking as his next of kin. He was in the second draft of the Yeomanry to go from Towcester to France on 21st February 1915. He was with the 5th District Police for a period in 1915.

According to the Yeomanry records, on 6th July 1915, targets were set up on the hill leading up to Mont de Cats, Boeschepe. 4 targets with a bull size of four inches at a range of 130 yards. Each soldier was given 10 rounds and Lewer scored 37. He was given leave from the front in May 1916 and again in August 1917.

THOMAS ARTHUR LUCK (1887-1976)

Thomas Luck's father also a Thomas married Thirza Rebecca (nee Pinney) in 1885, he died in 1887 and in 1891 she married Frederick Richardson. Thomas and his sister Sarah (who married Charles Jolley in 1906) were joined by seven other siblings from the marriage of Thirza and Frederick Richardson, of whom Frederick, Alfred and Charles Richardson, all fought in the war.

Thomas enlisted into the Northamptonshire Yeomanry (Private 1324) and was later transferred to the 7th Northamptonshire Regiment (Private 205821). None of his service records survive.

101

CHARLES SYKES MABBUTT (1878 – 1961)

Charles Sykes Mabbutt, the son of Charles and Elizabeth (nee Sykes), was born in Ecton. When he was twenty two he enlisted with the Royal Engineers (Sapper 7733) and served for 12 years. In 1901 and 1902 he served in South Africa receiving the Queen's South African medal with clasps for Cape Colony, Orange Free State and the Transvaal. He emigrated to Canada, his occupation given as carpenter. He returned to Canada after the war and worked as a logger. He died in December 1961.

In 1914 he enlisted into the Canadian Overseas Expeditionary Force at Valcartier Camp and was trans-shipped to England for further training, then on to the Western Front. He is registered on the 1918 Ecton Absent Voters List as serving in the 1st Field Company Canadian Engineers (1503).

THOMAS ERNEST MALLARD (1878-1939)

Thomas was the son of John and Hannah Mallard who lived in Back Street; John was a carter. Thomas started as an agricultural labourer but by 1911 was working as a road man. He married Ellen Spokes in 1903, they had two daughters and in 1911 were living in High Street, Ecton. Thomas died in 1939.

102

According to both the Roll of Honour and the Ecton War Book, Thomas enlisted in the Yorkshire Regiment. However there are no surviving records for him so it is impossible to verify this. Although he is mentioned in the Northamptonshire Yeomanry War Diary he could have first enlisted into the Yeomanry then been transferred to the Yorkshire Regiment. The 1918 Absent Voters List records Thomas as serving with the 667th Agricultural Company (Private 492349).

CHARLES WILLIAM MUNDON (1881-1946)

Charles was the son of William Henry Mundon and Georgina. William was a coachman working for the Sotheby family. Charles was born in Eaton Square Mews South, St. George, Hanover Square and became a groom, also working for the Sotheby family. In 1915 he married Mabel Anne Thurlby in Croydon, he died in Kensington age 65 in 1946.

Charles enlisted in the Army Service Corps (Private M2/053660) he went to France in March 1915 and was discharged in June 1919. There are no surviving records of his service.

JOHN MATTHEW PERKINS (1892-1965)

John was born in Blisworth the son of Cain and Ellen. In 1911 he was living in Ecton and working as a general carter for Alice

Randall. He was also one of the bell ringers although is not listed on the plaques in the Belfry. In 1913 he married Kate Pinney. After the war he worked as a leather dresser. He died in Northampton in 1965.

In 1914 John enlisted in the Royal Field Artillery (Corporal 43755) as a gunner and in October was serving in Salonica. He was later transferred to the Royal Garrison Artillery (174871, 1412654). No records of his service survive, he is registered on the 1918 Absent Voters List for Ecton as (Gr 186195) and on the 1919 list as serving in 1st Brigade Small Arms Artillery Company.

The Pinney Family

Frank and Frederick were the sons of Charles and Sophy (nee Liddington). The family lived in High Street, Ecton.

FRANK PINNEY (1889-1926)

Frank, born in Ecton 26th May 1889, was a member of the church choir and one of the Patriotic Bell Ringers although not on the photograph in the Belfry. He was also a scout master. Frank never married and he died in May 1926 aged 37 and is buried in Ecton Churchyard.

Frank enlisted in the Royal Army Medical Corps (Private 49257). He was promoted to Sergeant during his service. He went to France on 1st June 1915. Unfortunately no service records are available. He is on the 1918 Absent Voters List as a Sergeant with the 37th Field Ambulance Royal Army Medical Corps.

FREDERICK HAROLD PINNEY (1893)

Frederick was in the church choir and like Frank was one of the Patriotic Bell Ringers and he is on the Belfry photograph. He was confirmed in October 1909 and married Ada Tapp in 1924.

Frederick enlisted into the Army Service Corps as a Driver (Private 029166) on 15th December 1914 at Woolwich. He was with the British Expeditionary Force in France, 78th Field Ambulance 26th Division, embarking from Southampton on 18th September 1915, arriving at Le Havre on 19th. In January 1916 he embarked aboard the *SS Menominee* and arrived in Salonica on 16th January. In August 1916 he was admitted to hospital with a fever and again in October 1917. In November 1916 he was appointed Acting Corporal (with pay) and on the 1918 Absent Voters List is registered as being in the Heavy Transport Division.

Amongst the papers in his service record is a statement he wrote on the 5th September 1918, it states that when he was posted *his duty was to conduct the M.L.C. driver and the teams of mules through the*

105

ravine and up the hill to the saw-mill with the logs of timber which they were bringing in from the forest. After this to see the teams unhooked properly, watered and properly groomed and fed when the order was given. He reported that "on the 27.5.18 at about 1100hrs I was instructing an M.L.C. driver the correct way to groom when the mule kicked me in the testicles. The mule was a shy Barbary one. I was compelled to report sick at once."

The beginning of the statement is very difficult to decipher. The statement was sent to the ASC records at Woolwich from Salonica on 12th September 1918. Frederick is reported to have suffered bruising of the scrotum and testicle with the scrotum swollen three times normal size with blackish and purple discolouration of the skin.
Frederick was discharged on 17th April 1919 and lived in the village.

HERBERT CYRIL PINNEY (1895)

Herbert, a cousin of Frank and Frederick had moved with his parents Walter and Ellen to Birmingham and in 1911 was living in Adderley Road, Saltley, Birmingham. In 1911, age 16, he was a patient in the City Hospital. He worked with the Midland Railway in the Loco Department as a boiler washer. The family later moved back to The Crescent, Ecton. Herbert married Florence E. Wheeler in Greenwich in 1921.

On 11th of November 1915 Herbert enlisted as a Gunner in the 3rd Battalion Royal Garrison Artillery (Private 145437). He was in the reserve until 22nd March 1917 when he was posted for duty and went to Plymouth, from there in April to Gravesend and in May to Aldershot then in June to Bexhill. He left for France on 3rd July 1917 and was in the field by the 14th of that month. In May 1918 he reported sick having had a fall with a shell when on the guns which caused a hernia. He was sent to the No.12 Stationary Hospital at St. Pol, the No. 26 General Hospital in Etaples and on to the 3rd Military War Hospital in Exeter. On June 1st 1918 he was discharged and went back to duty and according to the Absent Voters List was in the 141st Siege Battery, Royal Garrison Artillery (Gnr 145437).

At his demobilisation on 10th September 1919 he was assessed as having a 20% disability from his hernia and was to be re- examined in 1920.

LEWIS PINNEY (1898-1976)

Lewis lived with his grandparents Thomas and Eliza Pinney in the High Street. He sang in the church choir and was confirmed by the Bishop of Peterborough in Weston Favell Church in June 1912. He married Mabel E. Spokes in 1924 and died in Northampton in 1976.

He enlisted in the Northamptonshire Regiment (Private 10355) and although there are no remaining service records the Ecton War Book states that he was wounded, it does not give any details. The Absent Voters List states in 1918 he was in the 6th Northamptonshire Regiment (Private 10369) and in 1919 he was in the 15th Loyal North Lancashire Regiment (45197).

GEORGE HENRY RANDS (1878-1955)

George Henry was the son of George and Eliza (nee Chapman), he was born in Preston Deanery, Northamptonshire. By 1891 the family had moved to Ecton with their three children, George Henry, Kate and Thomas Harry. George Henry married Alice Fuller in 1898 and in 1911 they were living in High Street, Ecton with their son George Edward. George Henry was a traction engine driver. According to the Ecton War Book, George Henry enlisted into the Army Service Corps Mechanical Transport and was promoted to sergeant. There is no existing medal card or army record for him. However the Absent Voters List for 1918 states he was in the Tractor Depot of the Army Service Corps (Sgt 099335).

After the war he and his son worked together farming in Ecton and George Henry became Chairman of the Parish Council. His son, George Edward married Suie M.Cave in 1933.

The Richardson Brothers

Alfred Albert, Charles and Frederick, were the sons of Frederick Richardson and his second wife, Thirza Rebecca, (Luck nee Pinney). In 1911 Frederick Richardson was described as a labourer on a farm. The family had moved from next to the Chapel in Back Street, where they had lived in 1901, to the High Street. Jean Leigh remembers Frederick as a market trader living on the corner of the A4500 and Wellingborough Road and having a market garden. Thirza's son from her first marriage, Thomas Luck, mentioned earlier, was also living with the family.

ALFRED ALBERT RICHARDSON (1893-1963)

Albert went into the Royal Navy serving on the HMS *Vanessa*. According to their records he received a war badge (no.1010) on 6th May 1917. In 1918 he was recorded on the Absent Voters List serving in His Majesty's Naval Base, Holyhead (Steward A.B.P.)

In 1920 Alfred married Emily A. Akehurst. He died in Northamptonshire in 1963, aged 70.

CHARLES JOHN RICHARDSON (1896-1978)

Charles was a member of the church choir and an altar server. He was confirmed on 20th October 1909 by the Bishop of Leicester in Earls Barton.

Charles joined the Navy as a signaller. He is registered on the 1918 Absent Voters List as serving in the R.N.V.R on H.M.S. *Roxburgh* (Sig 3900).

In 1928 Charles was working as a gardener in Weston Favell, he married Edna I. Kippin, a milliner. Charles died aged 80 in Northamptonshire in 1978.

FREDERICK WALTER RICHARDSON (1892-1979)

Like his two brothers, Frederick was also in the Royal Navy and is registered on the Absent Voters List as serving in the Royal Navy on H.M.S *Maidstone* (Sto. 29895).

He married Florence Eales in 1929. He died aged 83 in Northamptonshire in 1979.

The Robinson Brothers

Were the sons of Archibald and Mercy (nee Billson), Archibald's second wife. His first wife Eliza Jane (nee Billson) died in 1891 and in 1892 Archibald married her sister Mercy and they moved from the Post Office in Cogenhoe to Ecton. They lived in The Institute (now the Reading Rooms). Archibald worked as an insurance agent. He played the organ in the church and was the Parish Clerk. Three of their four sons fought in the Army and all returned home after the war.

ARCHIE ROBINSON (1895-1920)

Archie was born when the family were living in Cogenhoe. After they moved to Ecton he sang in the church choir and was confirmed in April 1910.

He enlisted in the Royal Army Medical Corps (Private 65864) and is registered on 1918 Absent Voters List serving in 103rd Field

Ambulance, Royal Army Medical Corps (Private 65864). On the 1919 list he is registered at Balcony House, Cromer.

<u>ARTHUR WILLIAM ROBINSON (1898-1986)</u>

Arthur, born in Ecton, was very involved in the church as a server a bell ringer and as the organ blower. He was confirmed by the Bishop of Peterborough in Earls Barton on 28th March 1911. He married Clara Kenning in Daventry in 1923 where he died in 1986.

He enlisted in the Northamptonshire Regiment and was taken prisoner on 9th May 1918 and ended the war in Germany. He is registered on the 1918 Absent Voters List as serving in the 2nd Northamptonshire Regiment (Private 27545)

ERNEST GEORGE ROBINSON (1892)

Ernest George, was the eldest of the Robinson brothers.

He enlisted in the Royal London Fusiliers (G/20453) he is registered on the 1918 Absent Voters List as serving in 25th Liverpool Regiment (Private 801499).

After the war he was living at 7 Faversham Avenue, Bush Hill Park, Middlesex, later he was thought to have moved to Nottingham.

ALBERT RODDIS (1878)

According to the Roll of Honour in the church Alfred Roddis was in the Canadian Force. This is possibly an error of transcription as there was no Alfred Roddis in Ecton but there was an Albert.

Albert Roddis lived in Back Lane, Ecton and he is registered on the 1918 Absent Voters List as serving in the 23rd Company Canadian Forestry Corps (101370).

FRANK SIMPSON (1887-1954)

In 1911 Frank was working as a shoe clicker (A shoe clicker is one of the top trades in the Northampton Boot and Shoe Industry) and living in Ecton with his grandmother. Frank was the son of William and Annie Elizabeth Simpson who were living in Earls Barton. In 1909 he married Alice Elizabeth the daughter of Frank and Sarah Johnson, Frank was the postmaster and father of the Johnsons mentioned earlier. Sadly Alice died in 1916 age 28 and in 1919 Frank married a second time, to Mary Jane Nevett. They lived in Brixworth where Frank died in 1954.

Frank enlisted in the 1st Battalion of the Northamptonshire Regiment (Private 8354). The Battalion went to France on 13th August 1914. He is registered on both the 1918 and 1919 Absent Voters Lists, in 1918 as Private 393953 and in 1919 as Private 303739 serving both years with the Army Service Corps Motor Transport Division. During his service Frank was wounded and discharged, he was awarded a Silver War Badge and returned home to England.

The Problem with the Smiths

There are so many Smiths of the same name and in the same regiments that it has been impossible to find out exactly who did what.

Albert and Frank were the sons of William and Amy Smith.
The family were born in High Beech, Essex and lived in Front Street, Ecton. William was a Steward on the Ecton Estate. Albert was working as a gardener's apprentice in 1891 then disappears from the Census records in Ecton. Frank was working as a carpenter in 1901 before he also disappears from the Ecton census after that date. William and Amy are recorded on the Parochial Electors list as still living in the village in 1921.

ALBERT EDWARD SMITH (1878)

According to the Roll of Honour he served in the Royal Engineers. There are no service records for Albert but he is registered on the 1918 Absent Voters List as serving in 402nd Royal Engineers (Spr. 222988).

FRANK ARTHUR SMITH (1879)

According to the Roll of Honour Frank served in the Essex Regiment.
Both Albert and Frank appear in the Ecton War Book, however they are not on the Absent Voters Lists.

FREDERICK ALFRED SMITH (1881)

Frederick was the youngest son of Charles and Mary Smith. Charles was a shoemaker and Frederick's occupation in 1901 was given as bricklayer. The family lived then in Chapel Yard, High Street , Ecton. Charles, Mary and Frederick Alfred were recorded on the Parochial Electors list for 1921.

According to the Ecton War Book and the Roll of Honour, Frederick served in the Royal Engineers. He is registered on the 1918 Absent Voters List as serving with the 411th Field Company, Royal Engineers (Cpl. 241250).

HERBERT WILLIAM SMITH (1891)

Herbert was the son of Charles and Annie Smith, he and his sister Ada were born in Ecton although their father was born in Brafield-on-the-Green and their mother in Great Billing. In 1911 Herbert's occupation was stone mason.

Herbert enlisted into the Warwickshire Regiment. Sadly there are no existing service records. However on the 1918 Absent Voters List he is serving in the 6th Warwickshire Regiment (Private 84589) and on the 1919 List in the Labour Corps (Private 34580).

Herbert married Lavinia Leach, the marriage was registered in Kettering in 1921 and Herbert died aged 73 in the same area in 1963.

The Sotheby Family in Ecton

The estate of the village of Ecton passed first to Charles Sotheby, then to his half-brother Major-General Frederick Edward Sotheby, the younger son of Admiral Charles Sotheby by his second wife. Frederick Edward enlisted in the Rifle Brigade, where commissioned at 18, he served in the Crimean War, the Indian Mutiny, the Chinese Wars and the Ashanti Wars. In his time in the village he donated the choir stalls in the chancel to the church, which he paid for with the exception of a small public subscription. He also enlarged the Lady Chapel and fitted it with seats and screens, dying in 1909 before it was completed. The Altar and Reredos were added in 1911 by his wife, Edith Marion, who inherited the estate for her life and in 1921 it passed to Lieutenant-Colonel Herbert George Sotheby, his nephew.

HERBERT GEORGE SOTHEBY D.S.O., M.V.O., D.L.
(1871-1954)

Herbert was the second son of Admiral Sir Edward Southwell Sotheby K.C.B. and Lucy Elizabeth Adeane. The family were landed gentry with a tradition of military and naval service. Lieutenant-Colonel Herbert George Sotheby had a distinguished military career, commissioned in the Argyll and Sutherland Highlanders, he fought in the Boer War and was wounded slightly on 1st January 1901 at Kroonstad whilst serving with the South African Field Force.

Herbert worked for the Royal Household as a clerk to the Privy Purse until the First World War.

In 1923 he married Marjorie Thompson (nee McCorquodale) widow of A.Y.Graham Thompson, a Captain in the Queen's Own Cameron Highlanders. They had no children and the estate at Ecton was to be left to their nephew, Lionel (who is commemorated on the shrine), eldest son of Herbert's elder brother William.

Herbert was promoted to Captain in 1902 and fought with Argyll and Sutherland Highlanders in the First World War. In 1916 he fought at the battles of Longueval, Bapume and on the Somme. In 1917 at Arras and Paschendaele. In 1918 he was at Amiens, Bapaume-Harleville, Epehy, Cambrai, St. Quentin, Selle River and at the capture of Avesnes-Mauberge.

118

He was promoted to Major in February 1916 serving with the 10th Battalion. In December that year he was promoted to Lieutenant-Colonel. [*Information extracted from the Royal Household Establishment Books 1526-1920).*

For his service Herbert received the D.S.O., Croix de Guerre (Gold Star), 1914 Star and British and Victory medals. During the course of the war he had been mentioned three times in despatches.

There were few changes made to Ecton Hall during his tenure and due to a dispute over death duties, with his brother William, he had to sell some of the property in the village. Up to that time the estate had owned almost the whole of the village with the exception of church property. He died at the age of 83 in 1954 and due to his nephew Lionel's death, at the battle of Loos, the estate passed to Lionel's younger brother Nigel.

NIGEL WALTER A. SOTHEBY (1897-1980)

Nigel, Lionel's younger brother, followed their paternal grandfather, Admiral Sir Edward Southwell Sotheby (1813-1902) into the Royal Navy. The Admiral had commanded the Pearl's Naval Brigade in the Indian Mutiny. Both he and Lieutenant-Colonel Herbert George, are buried in Ecton Churchyard.

119

Nigel served in the Royal Navy with the Dover Patrol aboard the HMS *Matchless*, HMS *Britannia* and HMS *Beaufort* rising to the rank of Lieutenant Commander.

He married Doris Lees in 1915 and inherited the Ecton Estate on the death of his uncle, Colonel Herbert Sotheby in 1954. Unfortunately he never lived there as, due to the heavy death duties, he had to sell the contents of Ecton Hall. This marked the end of centuries of employment in the village provided by the Sotheby family. Nigel died in Oswestry, Shropshire. Today Ecton Hall has been turned into luxury flats and the estate is managed by Fisher-German, for the Sotheby Family Trust.

WILLIAM EDWARD SOUTHWELL SOTHEBY (1866-1950)

William was the eldest son of Admiral Edward S. Sotheby and Lucy E (nee Adeane), he married Margaret Williams in 1894, she died in 1922. William then married Constance Alice J. Bradfield.
Lionel and Nigel were the sons of William's first marriage. The family were living in North Wales at the outbreak of the war in 1914. William died in Surrey in 1950 and was buried in Wales with his first wife.

William served in the British Red Cross Society as a Motor Ambulance Chauffeur. Using his own car and stationed in France at Boulogne-sur-Mer and later in the Balkans. Whilst in France he was

120

able to meet his son, Lionel on the occasions when Lionel was on leave from the Front.

Stopford-Sackvilles at The Hollies

Lionel Richard and Constance Evelyn (nee Gosling) were married in 1887 in Kensington. Constance was the daughter of Major George Gosling. After she was widowed Constance moved to The Hollies (now the Grange) in Church Way, Ecton. The family were related to the Isted family who preceded the Sothebys to the Ecton Estate.

Two of Lionel and Constance's sons, Lionel Charles and Geoffrey William are mentioned on the Roll of Honour in the church and Geoffrey, but not Lionel, is commemorated on the Shrine. The reason for this is that although they both died because of injuries sustained in the war, Lionel lingered until 1920 and by that time he had moved away from the village and was not included on the Shrine. The brothers were grandsons of Sackville George Stopford-Sackville, Drayton House, Northamptonshire.

LIONEL CHARLES STOPFORD-SACKVILLE (1891-1920)

Lionel was born on 30th April, 1891 in Belfast. He was a Captain in the 4th Battalion Rifle Brigade and during a distinguished military career, he received the Croix de Guerre (avec Palmes), the D.S.O.

and was awarded a Brevet Majority. He was Mentioned in Despatches in June and September 1915 and again in October 1917.

His conduct at the second Battle of Ypres and at St. Eloi won the approbation of his Colonel, Major-General George Thesiger.

His Majesty the King approved the awarding of the Companion of the Distinguished Service Order. This was recorded in the Supplement to the London Gazette 15th September 1915.

"For conspicuous gallantry and ability, since he obtained command of a Company in February 1915. Near Ypres, from 8th to 15th May, he did excellent work in the trenches, keeping up his men's spirits under very heavy bombardments. He took command of another Company in addition to his own, when it had lost all its officers. On the night of 14th/15th March, near St. Elio, he took a barricade with half his company, went forward by himself to reconnoitre, and then, returning for his company, led them back and cleared the houses on the road."

In December 1916 the same paper reported that he had been attached as Staff Captain to the 80th Brigade, a post he held until August 1917 when he was made Brigade Major to the 65th Brigade and held that appointment until August 1918. In the Supplement to the London Gazette, 18th July 1919, it states: *The President of the French Republic awarded the Croix de Guerre (avec Palmes) to Brevet Major L.C. Stopford-Sackville D.S.O. Rifle Brigade.*

On December 16th 1919, Rifle Brigade Captain and Brevet Major L.C. Stopford-Sackville D.S.O. retired on account of ill health contracted on active service.
He suffered from shell shock and was sent home in a serious condition in July 1918 and invalided out of the service in the December of that year, dying after months of suffering of slow paralysis on 31st December 1920. He is on the Roll of Honour in Ecton church.

ERNEST HENRY STUBBS (1891-1975)

Ernest Stubbs was born on 16th December 1891 in Northampton, he was the second son of William Stubbs and Matilda (nee Lee). In 1911 they were living at 9 Western Terrace, Northampton St. Peter. Ernest married Kate Clunie in Northampton in 1915 and he died in 1973 aged 82.

Ernest enlisted into the Northamptonshire Yeomanry (Private 1528, later changed to 1456777). Due to there being no existing service record or pension record it is not possible to detail his war service.

Ernest is mentioned on the Roll of Honour in the Church so may have moved into the village after his marriage. He is not mentioned in the Ecton War Book nor on the Absent Voters Lists for Ecton in 1918 and 1919.

The Sturman Brothers

Charles and Frederick were the sons of William and Mary Ann (nee Battisson) living in the Crescent in Ecton.

CHARLES WILLIAM STURMAN (1896 – 1971)

Charles enlisted into the 1/4 Battalion Territorial Force Northamptonshire Regiment (Private 2533) in late September 1914.

123

He embarked on the Troopship *Royal George* on 29th July 1915 for Gallipoli, eventually landing at Suvla Bay on 14th August. Returning to England due to enteric fever the following year, he was transferred to the 1st Battalion (Private 31111). The Ecton War Book mentions that he was taken prisoner by the Germans. The 1918 Absent Voters List has Charles registered in 1st Northamptonshire Regiment (Private 31111).

The Northampton Independent reports on 25th August 1917:
"Pte.C.W.Sturman of the Northamptons has been missing since the battle of the Dunes and his parents Mr. and Mrs.W.Sturman of Ecton, Northamptonshire, appeal for news of him. Pte.Sturman, who is 21 years of age, joined up in September 1914, fought in Gallipoli and was invalided home with enteric fever in February of the following year. On recovering he went out to France last November."

Charles married Beatrice H.M.Waples in 1921, he served in the Ecton No.6 Platoon Home Guard during the Second World War and he died in 1971.

FREDERICK ARTHUR STURMAN (1900)

A younger brother of Charles William, Frederick enlisted into the Middlesex Regiment, unfortunately no records of his service survive. The 1919 Absent Voters List registers Frederick at D.W.Bush

Camp, Pembroke Dock (Private 3375). *After the war he lived in the Crescent, Ecton, later moving to the cottages on Lower Ecton Lane. These cottages have been demolished to make way for development.*

JAMES CHARLES TANCRED (1865-1943)

Described in the Ecton War book as Captain, Royal Navy, he is not on the Roll of Honour as he wasn't a resident in the village. He was born in 1865. He was promoted to Captain on 1st January 1902.

In 1915 James Tancred was Captain on the *Argyll*. After being refitted at Plymouth the ship was expected to re-join her squadron at Rosyth. However as the North Sea was infested with German submarines it was decided the ship should sail clockwise round the British Isles. She sailed on the 25th October with 655 officers and ratings on board. The weather conditions were deplorable and the last natural hazard they had to contend with before reaching base was the Bell Rock. A request was made that the light from the lighthouse on the rock would be lit due to the appalling conditions. Unfortunately at that time the lighthouse could only be reached by visual signals or a visit by a motor boat. The motor torpedo boat sent with the message had to turn back after reaching the mouth of the Forth and a message was sent to the battleship *Queen Mary*, who replied that due to the weather they were unable to reach the lighthouse. No-one contacted the *Argyll* who sailed on. In the early hours of 28th October the weather lifted enough for the crew to see they were in a position which made it impossible to avoid the Bell

Rock. Despite the efforts of Captain and crew the ship wedged her keel amongst the rocks. The crew prepared to abandon ship, the lighthouse keepers were unaware that they had a ship stranded just below the lighthouse and although the crew tried to float a grass line to the lighthouse and get in touch with the keepers they were unable to do so. When the keepers showed their light at the routine time they at first thought the ship was German and hid. However, eventually reading the frantic signals they tried to float a line which succeeded and the crew of the ship attached a heavy hawser to it. The ship then received a signal informing her that lifeboats had been launched to come to the rescue and had been forced back but two destroyers were on their way to assist.

The crew promptly hauled the hawser back and as they did so the line caught round the leg of one of the keepers and dragged him to the floor and towards the entrance. Luckily, one of the other two keepers threw himself onto him holding him down, whilst the other managed eventually to cut the line. The crew on the *Argyll* unaware of the drama continued to haul in the line.

The destroyer *HMS Hornet* managed to get close enough to rescue 500 of the crew of the *Argyll* who had been assembled ready to abandon ship. The rest of the crew took to the lifeboats and rowed clear. The destroyer *HMS Jackall* rescued the remaining survivors from their lifeboats and by 12.30pm the entire crew was safely at Rosyth.

To prevent the *Argyll* becoming a wreck and a navigational aid for the enemy the Navy's salvage ship reduced her to a pile of scrap after removing everything of value.

The Targetts

Arthur Robert and Leonard Walter were the sons of Robert Walter and Mary Grace. Robert was the butler at Ecton Hall and Arthur had been born in Huntingdon during his father's previous post in Connington.

126

ARTHUR ROBERT TARGETT (1899-2000)

According to the Roll of Honour, Arthur enlisted in the Royal Naval Reserve (L.Z/6893) but according to the Ecton War Book he was a Telegraphist on the H.M.S. *Warspite,* the famous super dreadnought battleship, which left the Firth of Forth on 29th May 1916 for the battle of Jutland, where it received a hammering at "windy corner".

There are no surviving service records for Arthur Targett he is not mentioned on the 1918 or 1919 Absent Voters Lists. He married Amy Jones in Salford and died in Lancashire in 2000 aged 101

LEONARD WALTER TARGETT (1891-1973)

According to the Roll of Honour Leonard enlisted in the Royal Irish Rifles. There are no surviving records of his service. He and Arthur are at the bottom of the Role of Honour and out of sequence. Possibly they enlisted later in the war than the other men in the village. The 1919 Absent Voters List states Leonard was in the 2nd Northamptonshire Regiment (Private 70197).

On 25th March 1924 Leonard emigrated to Australia on the T.S.S. Hudsons Bay, landing at Freemantle. His occupation was given as farm hand and his residence in UK as Ecton.

The Tebby Brothers

Thomas and Elizabeth Tebby had eight children, four sons and four daughters. Thomas died in 1898 leaving Elizabeth to bring up the family on her own. She died in 1947.
Charles Christopher Tebby stayed in Ecton during the war working as a baker. He married Kate Esson, daughter of William and Alice Esson of Earls Barton. Charles and Kate's surviving daughter Jean Haycox is still living in the village.

BERTIE THOMAS TEBBY (1892-1978)

Bertie was a stoker working for the Nene Navigation Company when he was 19. At that time his three brothers were working around Ecton as farm labourers and they were all living at home with their mother. Bertie was one of the village's Patriotic Bell Ringers, whose photograph hangs in the church tower.

He joined the Northamptonshire Regiment (Private 20593). There are no service records and as his medal card doesn't state which battalion he was in it is difficult to say exactly where he served. Bertie is not on the Absent Voters Lists for 1918 or 1919.

Bertie married Florence Street in July 1914. He died in 1978 aged 87.

THOMAS HAROLD TEBBY (1897-1968)

Thomas Harold Tebby joined the Middlesex Regiment (G/34177). Again sadly there are no surviving service records for him. He is on the 1918 Absent Voters List recorded in 4th Middlesex Regiment (Private 34177).

In 1924 he married Elizabeth Norris Tibbs Smith, born in Kislingbury in 1899, the daughter of John and Edith Smith who were living in Ecton in 1911. Harold died in 1968.

HORACE TEBBY (1895-1975)

Horace worked for John Earl at Home Farm Ecton, the reference from John Earl sent to the Army stated that Horace was very good and straightforward in his work.

Horace enlisted into the Army Service Corps (Driver T3/029167) on 15th December 1914, he was nineteen years and seven months old. He went to France on the Troopship *Southampton* with the British Expeditionary Force on 25th March 1915 and disembarked at Le Havre. From there he was posted to the 28th Reserve Park.
On 8th February 1917 he was admitted to hospital with scabies, he returned to duty on 22nd and went to No. 1 Company 9th Division. During his service he earned a good conduct badge. However in July 1918 he forfeited two day's pay for being ten minutes late for roll call. Whilst in the army it is recorded he suffered from dental abscesses on more than one occasion. He was demobbed in May 1919. On the Absent Voters List for 1918 Horace is described as in 9th Divisional Train Army Service Corps (Dvr 3029167).

Horace returned to Ecton where in 1921 he married Elsie E. Harlott daughter of Herbert and Elizabeth of Front Street, Ecton. They had known each other all their lives and was the sister of his friend Frederick Harlott. Horace was also one of the Patriotic Bell Ringers, whose photograph hangs in the church belfry. He died in 1975.

130

The family in Rectory Farm

Bertie and Percy Timms were the sons of William and Frances *Timms. Their mother died in 1898 and in 1903 their widowed father married Clara Park, widowed mother of Thomas Gordon Park, commemorated on the Shrine. In 1911 William, Clara and William's daughter Frances and Clara's son Thomas were living in Rectory Farm, Ecton. Also living there was William's elder son from his first wife, William Thomas, his wife Geraldine Hilda Annie with their daughter, Lizzie Smith Timms aged 1.*

PERCY GEORGE TIMMS (1896-1963)

Percy was the younger brother of Bertie. In 1901 Percy was living with the family in the shop in Barnwell St Andrew village and moved to Mears Ashby in 1911 to work on Herbert Dunkley's farm.

Percy served in the Leinster Regiment (Private 5494) and the Royal Irish Fusiliers (Private 30497), there are no surviving records of his service. However according to the Ecton War Book, he was wounded twice and his Medal Card states that he also received a Silver War Badge and was discharged in 1918. *He married Annie Harper in 1920 and died in 1963 aged 67.*

__The Tiplers__
Thomas and Ann (nee Day)'s elder son, Henry, (born 1851) married Fanny the daughter of John and Sarah Smith of Rothersthorpe, in 1875. Henry and Fanny and their children, Sarah Jane, born in Ecton in 1877, Henry Edward born in Hardwick in 1879 and George Alfred born in Ecton in 1886 were living in Horse Shoe Yard.

GEORGE ALFRED TIPLER (1886-1976)

In 1911 George was living with his sister Clara and his widowed mother in the village, where he was working as a farm labourer.

On 13th November 1915 he enlisted at Kettering into the Northamptonshire Regiment (Private 235230) and was in reserve until 1916 when the Regiment were posted to France in the July. Two months later George was transferred to the Bedfordshire Regiment (Private 43394). On enlistment his address was given as Horse Shoe Yard, Ecton. He was 29 years and 8 months old, 5' 8" tall, his next of kin given as Fanny Tipler, Mother, of Horse Shoe Yard, Ecton.

As he was injured he was entitled to a pension, sadly his pension record is in a very poor condition and it is difficult to pin point when the injury occurred. However, with the Bedfordshire Regiment in France he would have been involved in a number of major battles, from Neuve Chappell in 1915 to the Spring Offensive on the Somme in 1918.

George sustained injuries to his arm at the beginning of 1918 and was discharged on 3rd June 1918 as unfit for active service. He was awarded the Silver War Badge.

According to the Ecton War Book, he was wounded badly in the arm, a piece of bone was transferred from his leg to his arm and as a result he partially regained the use of that arm. He was also granted a pension starting 29th May 1918, initially twenty seven shillings and sixpence for 4 weeks then reduced to eleven shillings. This was to be reviewed in 48 weeks from the time he was granted it.

In 1879 Thomas and Ann's younger son, Edward, married Lucy Jolley. Lucy was the daughter of Bailey and Elizabeth Jolley, living in Front Street, Ecton.
Edward and Lucy had two daughters, Selina (1880) and Clara Elizabeth (1883) and a son Harry Edward who is commemorated on the Shrine.

GEORGE TOWNLEY (1892-1977)

One of a large family, George was the eldest son of Frederick William Townley and Emily Louisa (nee Agutter).

133

George followed his father into the shoe trade and he also formed the 1st Earls Barton Scout Troop in 1909. He became a close friend of the Rev. Jephson and his wife in Ecton and they followed his subsequent career with interest. He would visit them when on home leave. George is in the Ecton War Book and a niece of his, Marion Gleave, is still living in the village.

George joined the 4th Northamptonshire Regiment on 9th September 1914, his brothers, Percy (East Surrey Regiment) and Fred (Lothian Regiment) followed him into the Army. From the moment George enlisted he kept a very detailed diary, covering his army training as a Signaller. Noting the first march, from Beyton to Thetford on 4th November, being 17 miles. Three days later he records being marched from Thetford to Bury St. Edmunds, a distance of 12 miles. Before being posted overseas George married Charlotte C. Whiting on Saturday 17th July 1915, in Earls Barton. On Wednesday 28th July he left St. Albans at 12.30am and sailed to the Dardanelles on the *H.M.S. Royal George*, embarking on 29th July 1915, together with 1/4 Northamptonshire Regiment, 54th Divisional Cyclist Company and 54 Divisional Royal Army Medical Corps. They were escorted by *H.M.S. Laverock*. In the Bay of Biscay he records what he called two memorable events being sea-sick and also seeing dolphins.

Arriving in Alexandria the men had a five mile march round the city accompanied by a band, a local policeman and a scout acting as their guides. From Alexandria they sailed via the Greek Archipelago to Suvla Bay, where they were given three days rations and a hundred extra rounds of ammunition, making two hundred and seventy rounds per man. They were landed at Kangaroo Point, Suvla Bay and immediately marched to the rear of the fighting line at the battle of Kidney Hill. They then moved during the next few days to support various other units. As a Signaller George was often on observation all night. He records that the first night's sleep he had since August 13th was on the 21st of that month.

Throughout all his time he was regularly receiving and sending letters and they seemed to get through, even in the most adverse of conditions. One food parcel which arrived contained a cryptic note – food spoilt by pears! Stationed nearby was a Sikh Regiment with whom they had very friendly relations. He became ill later in the year and was sent first to a hospital in Alexandria and then to Queen Mary's Military Hospital, Whalley, Lancashire. His diary stops at this point. After he recovered he went back to serve on the Western Front.

Before the War he had obtained a divinity scholarship to Lincoln College, Oxford and his first post after the war was Curate at Keighley, Yorkshire. He then went on to be Vicar of Lidget Green, Bradford, then Vicar of Linthorpe, Middlesborough, Rural Dean of Scarborough and finally Archdeacon of Cleveland before his elevation to the Episcopate as Suffragan to the Archbishop of York in 1957. The London Gazette Tuesday 9th April 1957 states that: "The Queen has been very pleased by Letters Patent under the Great Seal of the Realm, bearing the date the 5th instant, to nominate the Venerable George Frederick Townley, M.A., Archdeacon of York and Canon and Prebendary of Fenton in York Minster to be Bishop Suffagan of Hull in the Diocese of York."
In 1965 Bishop Townley retired and lived in Scarborough for a few years before returning to Earls Barton. (A true "Barton Leek") In 1970 he assisted the Rev. Nigel Abbott with the Earls Barton Parish Church Millennium celebrations of the Saxon Tower. Bishop Townley also served as an Assistant Bishop with the Peterborough Diocese until his death.

BENJAMIN WILKINS (1873-1937)

Benjamin was born in Farthinghoe, the son of George and Selina

(nee Mobbs), he married Temperance Wallinger in 1898 and they had three children, Marian O. born in 1900 and twins Emily Wallinger and Henry John born in January 1905. Benjamin died aged 64.

Benjamin was called up to serve in the 17th Battalion Essex Regiment (Private 56382) in June 1918 when he was 46 and it is recorded on his service record that it was after he had attained the age of 40. His civilian occupation was given as gardener. He was demobilised in January 1919. His service record is very brief. The 17th was a Home Service Battalion which remained in England.

Postscript:

From an article written by FRED JOHNSON

Writing about his memory of village life in 1978, Fred Johnson mentions that when he was at school a man who had been taken prisoner in WW1 had come into the class to talk about his experiences as a POW and Fred had found it rather gruesome. Unfortunately he doesn't say which of the returning prisoners of war went to the school.

A number of people in the village also remembered being told of German prisoners from the First World War working in the farms locally.

ECTON STRAYS

Whilst researching the men on the Roll of Honour, the Shrine and the Ecton War Book, the following people with Ecton connections came to light.

ARCHIBALD RODOLPH BARKER (1877)

Born in Ecton. In 1901 the family were living in Newington and Archibald was a Lieutenant in the Army. Records show he enlisted in the 72nd Company (Rough Riders), 20th Battalion Imperial Yeomanry (Private 16112). He received The Queen's South African Medal with clasps for Cape Colony, Orange Free State and Transvaal. Also the King's South African Medal with clasps, fighting in the Boer War 1901 and 1902.
There is a record of Archibald sailing to Halifax, Canada on the Corinthian in April 1911.

He enlisted into the Canadian Overseas Expeditionary Force in June 1915. His next of kin was given as his wife Winnifred, living at Hammer Farm, Shotterswell, Sussex, England. This was later amended to 1 Cylinder Cottages, Saltwood, Kent, England.

HARRY BAZELEY (1889)

Harry's parents Walter and Elizabeth lived in Front Street, Ecton where both Harry and his brother Frederick were born. Harry's occupation was farmer and he was 26 at the time of his enlistment.

Harry joined the Canadian Overseas Expeditionary Force on 27th December 1915. His next of kin was given as his elder brother Frederick Bazeley of The Island, Manitoba, Canada. His occupation was described as a farmer.

(Frederick sailed to Quebec in 1904. When aged 18, he had enlisted in the Royal Warwickshire Regiment and served in Africa from 1899 until 1902 and received the South African medal plus clasps for Belfast, Cape Colony, and Orange Free State.

According to the Canadian census of 1911 Harry had emigrated in 1908 and was living in Alberta working as a servant. He obviously visited England as he is recorded as sailing from Liverpool to Montreal in April 1913.

EDGAR CHARLES BAZELEY (1886), HERBERT BAZELEY (1889) and ALBERT WILLIAM BAZELEY,

The Bazeley brothers, the sons of Charles and Elizabeth, were all born in Ecton.
Before enlistment, Edgar had been working as a roadman and living with the family in Mears Ashby.
Edgar Charles enlisted in the Northamptonshire Regiment in September 1914 but was discharged in October as medically unfit, after serving 53 days.

Herbert was a farm labourer and played in the Mears Ashby football team.
In August 1915 he enlisted in the Northamptonshire Regiment (Private 15004) and was later promoted to Lance Corporal serving in France. *He married Rose Bell in 1914 and he died in 1968.*

Albert William also enlisted in the Northamptonshire Regiment (Private 19548). His service record has not survived.

BERTRAM BEESON (1894-1916)

Walking round Ecton Churchyard I noticed the grave of William Smithson, on the headstone is the name of his grandson Bertram Beeson who died in the battle of the Somme, September 6th 1916. Bertram was the son of Walter and Alice Beeson of 10 Pattison Road, Childs Hill, London.

In September 1914 he enlisted at 32, St. Paul's Churchyard, Middlesex into the Norfolk Regiment (Private 13866), he was later promoted to Lance Corporal. He was gassed at Hill 60 in September 1915 and is buried in Corbie Communal Cemetery Extension in France (Plot 1, Row C, Grave 24).

The cemetery is 15 kilometres from Amiens. During the battle of the Somme, Corbie became a medical centre. The communal cemetery was used until May 1916 when it became full and an extension was opened. The majority of the graves in this extension are of officers and men who died of wounds in the 1916 Battle of the Somme.

Bertram's mother was the daughter of William and Sarah Smithson, William was a coachman and he and Sarah lived in Front Street Ecton from 1901.

HARRY DOUGLAS BRITTEN (1890-1915)

Harry was born in Ecton and was the son of George and Emma Jane. In 1901 George was the licensed victualler of the Old White Horse Inn, High Street, Kettering.

Harry enlisted in the Household Cavalry and Cavalry of the Line (including Yeomanry and Imperial Camel Corps). His Battalion was the 3rd Dragoon Guards, Prince of Wales Own (Private 2590). He went to France on 31st October 1914 and was killed in action on 13th May 1915. He is remembered on Panel 3 of the Menin Gate Memorial at Ypres.

PHILIP CHAPMAN (1887-1918)

Philip, born in Ecton, was the son of Charles and Martha Chapman from West Dereham, Norfolk. His father was a farmer in Moulton.

Philip enlisted into the Bedfordshire Regiment in May 1915 (Private 20655). He later served with the 29th Middlesex (Private 72509) and in the 1st Battalion Cheshire Regiment (Private 50653). The Battalion served in France from 1914 to 1917 when they went to Italy. They returned to France in April 1918 and Philip was killed on 17th June 1918 and is remembered on the Ploegsteert Memorial (panels 4 and 5).

WALTER FLUTE

Walter Flute is recorded on the Electoral Roll, he was entitled to vote as a Parliamentary and Parochial Elector but not a County Elector. He was on the Occupation Electors list living at West Lodge. He was the son of William and Zipah Flute and he served in the Ox and Bucks Light Infantry (Private 27123) and then the South Wales Borderers (Private 40655).

FREDERICK CHARLES JOHNSON (1881-1951)

The eldest son of Charles and Rachel Johnson, had been a soldier in the Duke of Cornwall's Light Infantry enlisting in Northampton in December 1898 and going to South Africa in May 1901. He received the South African Medal in 1901-2 with clasps for Cape Colony, Orange Free State and Transvaal. He was discharged in 1909 as being unfit for further service. In 1911 Frederick was working as a painter in Derbyshire, where he married Elizabeth Hargreaves. He re-joined his old Regiment in 1915, and was posted to France on 21st May 1915. He died in Derbyshire in 1951. He is not mentioned on the Roll of Honour in the village or in the Ecton War Book as he was not living in the village when they were compiled.

WALTER PHILLIP STANNARD (1891)

Walter was the son of Ben and Eleanor (nee Patrick, born in Ecton). Ben was a bricklayer's labourer, the family moved frequently. Walter was born in Ecton.

Walter sailed to Halifax on 9th April 1908 and his occupation was logger, he was living at 358 Powell Street, Vancouver, British Colombia.

Walter enlisted in the Canadian Overseas Expeditionary Force on 4th January 1917, he was 25, and named his father, at that time living in Eden Street in Coventry, as his next of kin.

HENRY SUMMERFIELD (1885-1915)

Henry was the son of Sarah Summerfield, eldest daughter of John and Ann (nee Clarke). John was a shepherd and at the time of Henry's birth the family were living at 46 Front St. Ecton. Henry grew up within the family in Ecton, later living with his mother Sarah and step-Father Samuel Bettles in Kettering. His Aunt Ada married Joseph Bearles, a boot leveller living in Kettering. Henry moved in and boarded with them. He was working as a leather clicker. (One of the top trades in the Northampton Boot and Shoe Industry).

Henry enlisted in the Northamptonshire Regiment on 14th December 1915 aged 30 (Private 22766). According to the service records he committed suicide whilst temporarily insane on 16th December 1915. A letter included in his service record says:

"To the Adjutant, The Depot, Northamptonshire Regiment.
Sir.
On the afternoon of the 15th December 1915 No 22766 Pte H.Summerfield reported himself at the recruiting offices at 36 Style Street Kettering. He was paid two day's pay which was due to him and sent home. Having been told to parade at 9 o'clock the following morning. He apparently seemed rather depressed and left repeating that he would never make a soldier. After arriving home he went upstairs and changed into civilian clothes. He then went out. As he didn't return his people reported the matter to the Police. On the morning of the 16th of Dec. 1915 he was found by the Police in a well at the back of his house in 75 Edmund Street, Kettering but some distance away. He was quite dead in about 3 feet of water. I attended the inquest which was held this afternoon at the Bucclaugh Hotel Kettering. A verdict of suicide whilst temporarily insane was given. All his military kit will be sent to OC A Coy. tomorrow except his shirt which could not be taken off him owing to the position he was in."
He is buried in Kettering (London Road) Cemetery and although listed in the Commonwealth War Graves Registers he is buried near the Cross of Sacrifice in a family grave not a war grave. The headstone reads: In ever loving memory of our beloved son Henry Summerfield departed this life December 16th 1915 aged 30 years. The headstone also records his Half- sister and Step-father

CHARLES HENRY TAPP (1891 - 1946)

. (Photograph courtesy of David Dicks).

Although not born in Ecton, Charles Henry Tapp merits a mention in this book because he was a bell ringer in Ecton Church up to the war and in 1913 he married Clara Elizabeth Tipler in Ecton Church. They lived in Great Billing and later moved to Ecton where their son Teddie was born. Charles worked at Manor Farm as a horseman, Clara died in 1940 and in 1941 Charles married Emily Isabella Barker. He served on the Ecton Parish Council for many years until his death. He and Emily are buried in Ecton Churchyard. Charles served in the Coldstream Guards (Private 5138). According to his medal records he qualified for the 1914 Star on 11th September 1914.

The Coldstream Guards formed their 4th (Reserve) Battalion in August 1914 this changed in July 1915 to the 5th (Reserve) Battalion, who did not leave England but provided drafts of men throughout the war. In total they sent around 16,860 men from all ranks. In July 1915 a 4th (Pioneer) Battalion was formed and left for the front. At the outbreak of war the Coldstream Guards were amongst the first British regiments to arrive in France. They suffered heavy losses and at the first Battle of Ypres the 1st Battalion was virtually wiped out. They fought in Mons, Loos, Somme, Ginchy and the 3rd Battle of Ypres.

APPENDIX I

SERVICE MEDALS

Each soldier, sailor and airman who served in a defined theatre of war against Germany and her allies was entitled to one or more campaign medals. Medals were sent to the next of kin where a recipient had been killed.

THE 1914 STAR
Awarded to those who served in France or Belgium between August 5th and midnight on 22/23rd November 1914. Where they were within range of enemy guns a bronze bar was awarded and this was attached to the medal ribbon. It is popularly referred to as the Mons Star. Men who did not leave the rear areas were not entitled to the bar.

THE 1914-15 STAR
Awarded to those who served in France or Belgium, after 23rd November 1914 but before December 1915, similar to the 1914 Star. It was never awarded with the bar, to distinguish those who served under fire.

Only one star could be held and members of the Royal Navy could only receive the 1914-15 Star if they served ashore in France or Belgium before 23rd November. The Royal Naval Division fighting on shore in Antwerp were eligible.

As well as receiving one of the Stars, members of the services would also be awarded two further campaign medals.

THE BRITISH WAR MEDAL
The medal was awarded for eligible service to service personnel and civilians alike. Qualification for the award varied slightly according to service. The basic requirement was they either entered a theatre of war or rendered approved service overseas between 5th August 1914 and 11th November 1918. Service in Russia in 1919 and 1920 also qualified. The medals are all dated 1914-1918. People sent abroad on or after 1st January 1916 were only eligible for this and the Victory Medal.

THE VICTORY MEDAL
This medal commemorated the Allied Victory. The medals are inscribed around the rim with the name, regiment and regimental number of the

recipient. It was not necessary to claim a medal as they were automatically sent to the last known address of the serviceman.

DEAD MAN'S PENNY
Where someone had been killed two further items were sent to the next-of-kin, a large bronze plaque known as the Dead Man's Penny, this was instituted in 1916 when the British Government decided that they needed some form of official token of gratitude to be given to fallen servicemen and women's next of kin. It is a twelve centimetre disc cast in bronze gunmetal, incorporating an image of Britannia and a lion, two dolphins representing Britain's sea power and the emblem of Imperial Germany's eagle being torn to pieces by another lion. Britannia is holding an oak spray with leaves and acorns. Beneath this is a rectangle for the recipient's name. No rank was given, to show equality in death. On the rim are the words *"He (or She) died for freedom and honour"* a scroll accompanied the plaque this was individually named with rank and regiment,

TERRITORIAL FORCE MEDAL
The medal was only awarded to members of the Territorial Force. To qualify they had to have been a member of the Territorial Force on or before 30th September 1914 and to have served in an operational theatre of war between 5th August 1914 and 11th November 1918.

THE SILVER WAR BADGE
The Silver War Badge (SWB), erroneously called The Silver Wound Badge, was authorised in September 1916 and is a circular badge with "For King and Empire-Services Rendered" surrounding the George V cypher. The badge was awarded to those military personnel who were discharged as a result of sickness or wounds contracted during the war either at home or overseas. It was to be worn "On the right breast or right lapel of the jacket but not on Naval or Military uniform" the Silver War Badge was awarded to medically unfit soldiers so they would not be branded cowards or conscientious objectors when they were seen to be wearing civilian clothes during the duration of the war.

MILITARY and DISTINGUISED CONDUCT MEDALS
The Military Medal was instituted on March 25th 1916, awarded for bravery in the field by other ranks, not officers. The medal bore the name, rank, number and unit on the rim and bars were awarded for additional acts considered medal worthy. It is for lesser acts of bravery than the Distinguished Conduct Medal. These awards were published in the London Gazette. George Harsent received the Military medal and this was recorded in the Regiment's War Diary.

DISTINGUISHED SERVICE ORDER

Awarded to officers of major (or equivalent rank) and above for distinguished services under fire. The details of this award were published in the London Gazette. Lionel Stopford-Sackville was a recipient.

MENTIONED IN DISPATCHES

Lionel Southwell Sotheby and both Geoffrey and Lionel Stopford-Sackville were named in their commander's despatch to higher authority and this was published in the London Gazette. This 'reward' could be made posthumously and to symbolise this award a sprig of bronze oak leaves was worn on the ribbon of the Victory Medal and a special certificate was issued.

APPENDIX II

THE PATRIOTIC BELL RINGERS

An article in the Northampton Independent dated January 16th 1915 shows a photograph which is hanging in the belfry in the church of St. Mary Magdalene in Ecton. It is entitled "THE PATRIOTIC BELL RINGERS" and lists Frank Pinney R.A.M.C., Frank Johnson, Bert Johnson and Fred Harlott all in the Northamptonshire Yeomanry, Fred Pinney and Horace Tebby in the Army Service Corps. The article goes on to say that 29 men from Ecton had joined up to date and that represented 6% of the population of 506.

(Courtesy of Northampton Newspapers).

INDEX – NAMES

Flute, Walter – 140
Flute, William and Zipah - 140
Fortune, Eleanor E. (nee Gibbons) - 76
Fortune, John Michael - 76
Fortune, Patrick and Charlotte - 76
Freeman, Charles - 77
Freeman, Esther Irene (nee Tebby) – 77
Freeman, Gladys Irena - 77
Freeman, William and Mary (nee Jellis) – 77
Freeman, William Thomas - 77
French, Field Marshal, Sir John – 38, 47

Garley, Anny - 27
Garley, George - 27
Garley, Jim - 27
Garley, John - 27
Garley, John Thomas – 13, 16, 26, 27
Garley, Lillie E. (nee Randall) – 26
Garley, Lilly - 27
Gleave, Marion – 4, 134
Gosling, Major George - 121
Gray, Andrew Young – 78, 79, 100
Gray, Edith Minna (nee Summerfield) - 79
Gray, William and Margaret (nee Young) – 78, 79
Green, Mr. – 100
Grey, Albert Victor – 79, 80
Grey, Nathaniel and Ethel Mivera (nee Barritt) - 79
Groom, Henry – 59

Hall, James Thomas and Nanny Stevens Hall - 80
Hall, John Henry – 80
Hall, Lily - 80
Hall, Marjorie - 80
Harlott, Constance - 81
Harlott, Daniel and Lucy (nee Randall) – 81
Harlott, Elsie – 81,
Harlott, Elsie (nee Tebby) - 130
Harlott, Elizabeth – 81, 130
Harlott, Elizabeth (nee Tebbutt) – 81
Harlott, Evelyn (nee Robinson) - 81
Harlott, Frederick Walter – 81, 82, 87, 130
Harlott, Geoffrey Walter – 4, 81
Harlott, Gwendolene – 81
Harlott, Herbert F. - 81
Harlott, Herbert John – 81, 130
Harlott, Leonard J – 81
Harlott, Winifred – 81
Harsent, Edith Annie (nee Hensman) – 83
Harsent, Elsie - 83

154

REGIMENTS

MEMORIALS & CEMETERIES

BIBLIOGRAPHY

Assorted Contributors to The Great War - a history in nine volumes
Baker, Chris – The Battle for Flanders
Bridger, Geoff - The Great War Handbook
Chapman, Stuart – Home in Time for Breakfast
Coltman, William – The Story of Two Crosses
Coombes, Rose E.B. – When Endeavours Fade
Coppart, George – With Machine Gun to Cambrai
Evans, Martin Marix – 1918, The Year of Victories
Foley, Michael - Hard as Nails The Sportsmen's Battalion of World War One
Hamilton, Andrew & Reed, Alan - Meet At Dawn Unarmed
Higgins, Thomas James – Tommy at Gommecourt
Holland, Chris and Phillips Rob – Fred C.Tracey, Not Such a Bad Time
Holloway, W.H. – Northamptonshire and The Great War
Holmes, Richard - The Western Front
Holmes, Richard – Soldiers
Holmes, Richard – The Little Field Marshal
Holmes, Richard – Tommy
Ingram, Rodney - Ecton a Northamptonshire Parish
James, Brig. E.A. - British Regiments
Lynch, E.P.F. -Somme Mud
Macdonald, Lynn –Somme
Masters, John – Fourteen Eighteen
Middlebrook, Martin – The Kaiser's Battle
Middlebrook, Martin - Your Country Needs You
Mitchell, Jeremy – Shrapnel and Whizzbangs
Morgan, Harry – "Our Harry's" War
Murland, Jerry – Departed Warriors
Northamptonshire Independent Newspaper
Peat, Harold – Private Peat
Richter, Donald - Lionel Sotheby's Great War
The Burgoyne Diaries
Townley, George, Diaries - courtesy of Marion Gleave

Ward, Alec -A Young Man's War, courtesy of Vicki Jaffe
Westlake, Ray - Kitchener's Army
Westlake, Ray - Tracing British Battalions on the Somme